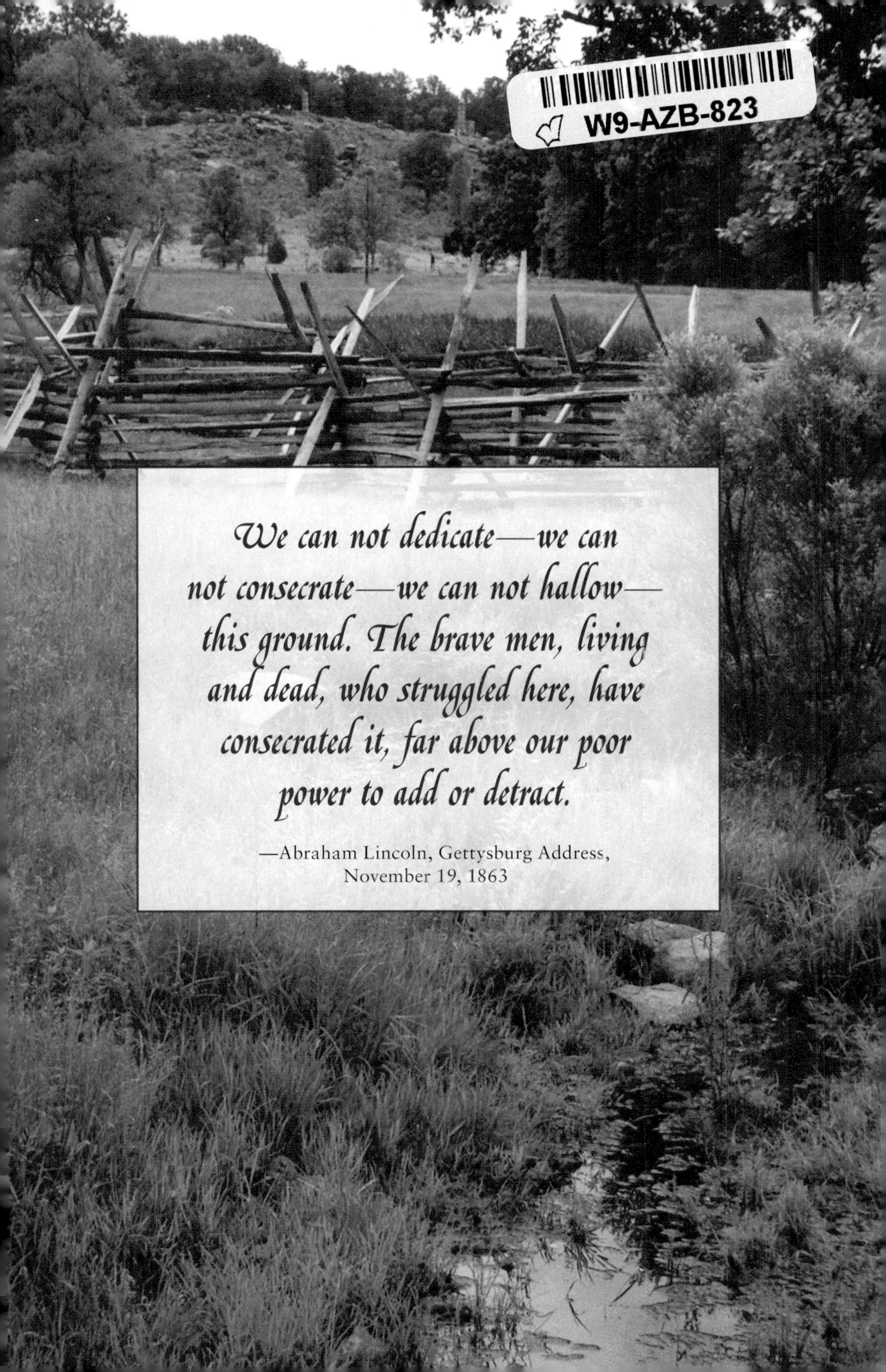

We can not dedicate—we can not consecrate—we can not hallow—this ground. The brave men, living and dead, who struggled here, have consecrated it, far above our poor power to add or detract.

—Abraham Lincoln, Gettysburg Address, November 19, 1863

72ND PENNA INFANTRY

GETTYSBURG

NATIONAL MILITARY PARK

MUSEUM AND VISITOR CENTER

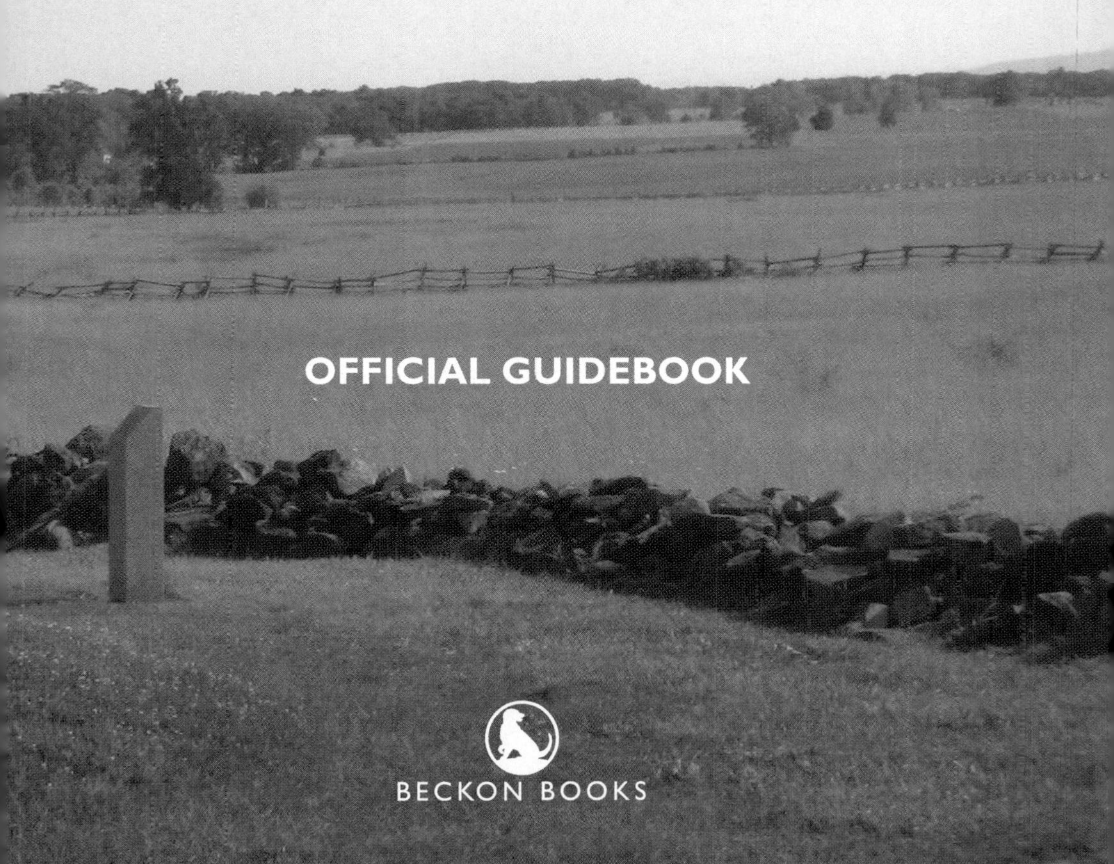

OFFICIAL GUIDEBOOK

BECKON BOOKS

Welcome to Gettysburg

At Gettysburg, the Union experienced monumental struggles and acts of bravery—acts that helped forge America's identity. Today, Gettysburg has much to offer, from the Cyclorama, Film, and Museum Experience at the Gettysburg National Military Park Museum and Visitor Center, to the battlefield tours, to the numerous historic sites around the town and battlefield.

Gettysburg National Military Park is a unit of the National Park Service that preserves and protects the resources associated with the Battle of Gettysburg and the Soldiers' National Cemetery, and provides an understanding of the events that occurred there within the context of American history. The Gettysburg Foundation is a non-profit educational organization working in partnership with the National Park Service to enhance preservation and understanding of the heritage and lasting significance of Gettysburg. In addition to operating the Gettysburg National Military Park Museum and Visitor Center, the Foundation has a broad preservation mission that includes land, monument, and artifact preservation, and battlefield rehabilitation—all in support of the National Park Service's goals at Gettysburg.

We hope that during your visit you'll take the time to experience all of Gettysburg. In doing so, you will gain a better understanding of Gettysburg's history, and the importance of preserving, enhancing, honoring, and protecting one of America's most significant places.

The Battle of Gettysburg

Many consider the Battle of Gettysburg to be a turning point in the American Civil War (1861–1865). It brought the Union a much-needed victory, and it put the South on the defensive, ending General Robert E. Lee's second and most ambitious invasion of the North. Often referred to as the "High Water Mark of the Rebellion," it was the war's bloodiest battle with 51,000 casualties (killed, wounded, captured, or missing). The extent of sacrifice at Gettysburg was, and still is, unprecedented in American history. More men fought—and died—during the Battle of Gettysburg than in any other battle before or since on American soil.

From July 1 to July 3, 1863, Gettysburg was a place of conflict. In the decades following, it became a symbol of reconciliation. At Gettysburg, Abraham Lincoln helped heal a battered nation with his famous Gettysburg Address. And at Gettysburg, soldiers from both sides returned not to fight, but to shake hands on the battlefield that changed their lives.

Today, Gettysburg symbolizes the utmost in patriotism as a place where all Americans can honor the soldiers in Blue and Gray. Thanks to veterans and other concerned citizens, nearly 1,400 monuments and memorials have been erected to honor the brave, true heroes of America. As President Lincoln stated, it is "a final resting place for those who here gave their lives that the nation might live."

Planning Your Visit

Millions of people have visited Gettysburg, and many return again and again. To get the most out of your visit, plan your trip in advance at www.gettysburgfoundation.org. There, you can purchase tickets—including value packages for the Cyclorama, Film, and Museum Experience and battlefield tours—and read about the history and preservation of the battlefield.

Little Round Top: The memorial to the 44th and 12th New York Infantry, located on Little Round Top, is the largest regimental monument in the park. It stands 44 feet tall and 12 feet wide in honor of the two New York regiments that helped defend the hill.

Once you've arrived, start at the Gettysburg National Military Park Museum and Visitor Center. Located at 1195 Baltimore Pike just south of historic downtown Gettysburg, the center features the exclusive Cyclorama, Film, and Museum Experience. This includes the Morgan Freeman–narrated film *A New Birth of Freedom* (sponsored by The History Channel); the massive Cyclorama painting, which literally surrounds guests with the fury of Pickett's Charge; and a museum of 12 exhibit galleries that contain artifacts and interactive displays.

The Museum and Visitor Center offers a variety of information on tours and other activities. From the center, you can plan your battlefield tour by choosing from several options: a bus tour with one of Gettysburg's renowned Licensed Battlefield Guides; a personal tour in your own vehicle with a Licensed Battlefield Guide; an auto CD tour, available for purchase in the Museum Bookstore; or a self-guided auto tour following the park's official road map and guide. The Museum and Visitor Center can provide you with maps of the battlefield walking trails. It also sells tickets for President Eisenhower's Gettysburg home—now the Eisenhower National Historic Site—and the David Wills House downtown (another National Park Service site). In addition, the Center provides schedules and information on a variety of ranger-led programs through the National Park Service. These programs are offered during the summer, fall, and spring, and several run daily. To download schedules and find out more details, visit www.gettysburgfoundation.org or www.nps.gov/gett.

While you're at the Museum and Visitor Center, take some time to sample Civil War-era food in the Refreshment Saloon—modeled after the saloons that offered snacks and other items to Civil War troops—and to visit the Museum Bookstore. The bookstore features a wide selection of books and souvenirs. (You can also shop online at www.gettysburgfoundation.org.) Friends of Gettysburg members receive a discount in the Museum Bookstore. Proceeds from all purchases made in the Museum and Visitor Center—including tickets—benefit battlefield preservation.

Museum and Visitor Center: Completed in 2008, the Gettysburg National Military Park Museum and Visitor Center features the exclusive Cyclorama, Film, and Museum Experience, which educates visitors on the Civil War and the importance of the Battle of Gettysburg.

The town of Gettysburg features a host of accommodations and amenities. At www.gettysburgfoundation.org, you will find a list of businesses that partner with the Foundation through the Friends of Gettysburg Business Partner Program and the Ticket Partner Program. For additional information on planning your visit, contact the Gettysburg Convention & Visitors Bureau in the lobby of the Museum and Visitor Center or go to www.gettysburg.travel.

Gettysburg offers a lot to do for everyone. Below is a sample itinerary to help you plan your visit.

Day One:

Film and Cyclorama • *1 Hour*

First, see the Morgan Freeman–narrated film *A New Birth of Freedom*, which sets the stage for the whole Gettysburg experience. After the film, make your way to the Cyclorama painting platform. The Cyclorama painting includes a sound and light show that immerses visitors in the fighting of Pickett's Charge and describes the history of the painting and battle. Visitor services representatives are also on hand to answer questions.

Snack

After the film and Cyclorama, head downstairs and sample some period food in the Refreshment Saloon, modeled after an actual Civil War-era saloon.

Battlefield Tour • *2.5 Hours*

If you haven't already booked your battlefield tour, visit the ticket counter in the Museum and Visitor Center, where you can choose from a bus tour with a Licensed Battlefield Guide; a private tour (in your car) with a Licensed Battlefield Guide; an auto CD tour, available for purchase in the Museum Bookstore; or a self-guided auto tour following the park's official road map and guide. Licensed Battlefield Guides train for years and must pass extensive tests to qualify to give tours. Bus tours and car tours with Licensed Battlefield Guides get booked quickly, especially during the summer months. Schedule yours in advance by booking online at www.gettysburgfoundation.org or by calling the advance sales department toll free at 877-874-2478. Please note that you should reserve your Licensed Battlefield Guide at least three days in advance.

Museum • *1.5–2 Hours*

Return to the Museum and Visitor Center and spend some time exploring the museum. Inside are interactive and multimedia exhibits, short films, artifacts, and information about the Civil War and Battle of Gettysburg.

Museum Bookstore

Browse the extensive selection of Gettysburg and Civil War–era books and souvenirs. The bookstore contains Civil War–themed field maps, history books, music and DVDs, clothing and jewelry, posters and prints, mugs, and even toys and games for kids.

Day Two:

Museum and Visitor Center • *1–3 Hours*

Stop at the information desk to check the schedule of National Park Service Ranger programs. Numerous programs are offered each day during the summer, including battlefield walks, where you can hike the trails on the 6,000-acre battlefield. You can also walk the fields from Seminary Ridge to Cemetery Hill, where thousands of Confederates attacked the Union line on the third day during Pickett's Charge.

The Soldiers' National Cemetery • *1 Hour*

See where Abraham Lincoln gave the Gettysburg Address and reflect on the

soldiers who fought at Gettysburg. National Park Service Ranger–led walking tours are available seasonally; information is available at the Ranger desk in the Museum and Visitor Center and online at www.nps.gov/gett. You can even walk to the cemetery by parking your car at the Museum and Visitor Center and following the clearly marked trail.

Eisenhower National Historic Site • *1.5–2 Hours*

Visit the only home President Eisenhower ever owned, located right by the Gettysburg battlefield. From the Museum and Visitor Center, you can purchase shuttle and admission tickets to the Eisenhower home. Once there, you can tour the former president's home, take a self-guided walk around the farm (home to black Angus cattle and several endangered species), or hear a National Park Service Ranger discuss 1950s Secret Service operations and Eisenhower's role in World War II.

David Wills House • *1-1.5 Hours*

Go to the National Park Service museum located at 8 Lincoln Square in downtown Gettysburg, where Abraham Lincoln put the finishing touches on the Gettysburg Address. There, you'll learn about the aftermath of the Battle of Gettysburg, the establishment of the Soldiers' National Cemetery, and Lincoln's trip to the Wills House. Shuttle service and shuttle tickets are available from the Museum and Visitor Center.

Remember, proceeds from all purchases in the Museum and Visitor Center—including tickets—benefit battlefield preservation.

Weather The summer months can be hot and humid, with occasional severe thunderstorms. Fall and spring are pleasant with cool temperatures and brisk winds. Winter weather occasionally forces the closure of some park roads and buildings.

Little Round Top: A statue of Union General Gouverneur K. Warren stands at the summit of Little Round Top. On July 2, Warren climbed to the top of the hill and spotted Confederate troops massing for an attack. He rallied Union troops and saved the left flank of the Union army.

Personal Items Dress appropriately so you can enjoy the grounds when weather permits. Bring hiking boots, sunscreen, and extra water. If you plan to participate in Ranger-led walks, bring bug spray.

Backpacks Backpacks, large handbags, large containers, and large parcels are not permitted inside the Museum and Visitor Center. Please stow these in the trunk of your vehicle.

Strollers Strollers are not allowed in the film theaters or the Cyclorama gallery. Stroller parking is available outside the entrance to the film theaters.

Food Food is available in the Refreshment Saloon. Because of health-department regulations, food prepared outside the facility is not permitted inside the saloon. Picnic areas are available outside. Please note that food and beverages are not allowed in the museum galleries, the theaters, or the Cyclorama gallery.

Pets Leashed pets are allowed on the grounds of the park but not in the park buildings or in the Soldiers' National Cemetery. Only service animals will be admitted into the Museum and Visitor Center.

These venerable men . . . were willing to die that the people might live . . . Their work is handed unto us, to be done in another way, but not in another spirit.

—President Woodrow Wilson, on the 50th anniversary of the battle, July 4, 1913

Accommodations for Visitors with Special Needs The Museum and Visitor Center is a handicapped-accessible facility. The park offers wheelchairs upon request, as well as assisted-listening devices for the film *A New Birth of Freedom* and the Cyclorama presentation.

Advance Tickets Purchase tickets in advance for the Cyclorama, Film, and Museum Experience, battlefield tours, and the Eisenhower National Historic Site at www.gettysburgfoundation.org. Groups of 16 or more visitors should make advance reservations by calling the Group Sales department at 877-874-2478.

At Gettysburg National Military Park, driving tours—by horse and car—have been popular for more than a century. Today, the park offers several ways to tour the 6,000-acre battlefield: by bus or by car with a Licensed Battlefield Guide, using the auto CD tour (available for purchase in the Museum Bookstore), or following the self-guided auto tour on the park's official road map and guide (pictured opposite).

The Battlefield: By touring the battlefield at Gettysburg National Military Park, visitors can gain a better understanding of what remains the largest battle ever fought on the continent.

The 24-mile auto tour starts at the Museum and Visitor Center and weaves through the town and battlefield. More than 60 percent of the buildings from the time of the battle are still standing, and nearly 1,400 monuments and memorials dot the landscape. The self-guided auto tour includes 16 stops, as indicated by the red numbers on the map. Each tour option takes approximately two and a half hours to complete.

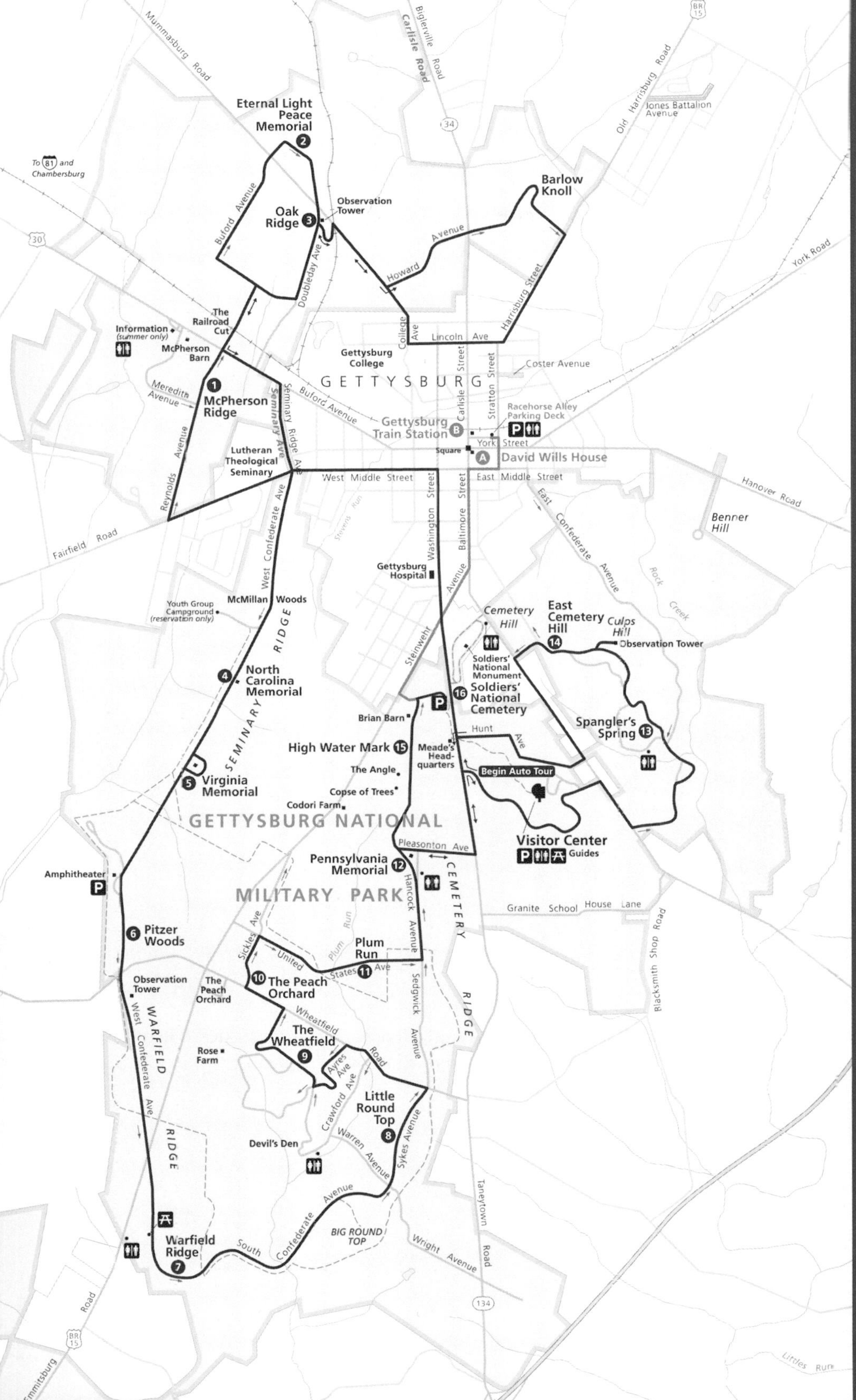

Mummasburg Road
Biglerville Road
Carlisle Road
Old Harrisburg Road
Jones Battalion Avenue
Eternal Light Peace Memorial
2
To 81 and Chambersburg
Oak Ridge
3
Observation Tower
Buford Avenue
Doubleday Ave
Howard Avenue
Barlow Knoll
York Road
Harrisburg Street
30
34
The Railroad Cut
Information (summer only)
McPherson Barn
College Ave
Lincoln Ave
Gettysburg College
Coster Avenue
GETTYSBURG
1
McPherson Ridge
Meredith Avenue
Seminary Ave
Seminary Ridge Ave
Buford Avenue
Carlisle Street
Stratton Street
Racehorse Alley Parking Deck
Gettysburg Train Station
B
York Street
Square
A
David Wills House
Reynolds Avenue
Lutheran Theological Seminary
West Middle Street
East Middle Street
Hanover Road
East Confederate Avenue
Benner Hill
Fairfield Road
West Confederate Ave
Washington Street
Baltimore Street
Stevens Run
Rock Creek
Gettysburg Hospital
Youth Group Campground (reservation only)
McMillan Woods
SEMINARY RIDGE
Steinwehr Avenue
Cemetery Hill
East Cemetery Hill
14
Culps Hill
Observation Tower
Soldiers' National Monument
4
North Carolina Memorial
16
Soldiers' National Cemetery
Spangler's Spring
13
Brian Barn
Hunt Ave
High Water Mark
15
Meade's Headquarters
The Angle
Begin Auto Tour
5
Virginia Memorial
Copse of Trees
Codori Farm
GETTYSBURG NATIONAL
MILITARY PARK
Visitor Center
Guides
Pleasonton Ave
Pennsylvania Memorial
12
Amphitheater
Hancock Avenue
CEMETERY RIDGE
Granite School House Lane
6
Pitzer Woods
Sickles Ave
Plum Run
United States Ave
11
Blacksmith Shop Road
Observation Tower
The Peach Orchard
10
The Peach Orchard
Wheatfield Road
West Confederate Ave
WARFIELD RIDGE
The Wheatfield
9
Sedgwick Avenue
Rose Farm
Ayres Ave
Crawford Ave
Little Round Top
8
Warren Avenue
Sykes Avenue
Devil's Den
South Confederate Avenue
Taneytown Road
BIG ROUND TOP
Warfield Ridge
7
Wright Avenue
134
Emmitsburg Road
15
Littles Run

The Cyclorama and Film

Before movies or television, cycloramas brought images to life for audiences around the world. These vast circular paintings thrust viewers into the middle of battles, religious epics, natural disasters, and scenes from great works of literature. Lighting effects on canvas and a narrated script gave the illusion of movement. And rocks, weapons, and other objects placed in the foreground provided a sense of depth. Hundreds of cycloramas were painted and exhibited in Europe and America during the 1800s. Most were lost or destroyed as their popularity died out at the turn of the century with the advent of movies.

Confederate Cannon: The Cyclorama painting captures cannon on the fields of Pickett's Charge—a nod to the massive artillery bombardment that preceded the Confederate attack on the Union's center line.

French artist Paul Philippoteaux completed the *Battle of Gettysburg* in 1884. Philippoteaux was a prolific artist who created at least eight cycloramas during the late 1800s on subjects ranging from Niagara Falls to Egyptian battlefields. For the *Battle of Gettysburg*, he carefully studied the battlefield, assisted by a battlefield guide and a photographer, and interviewed a number of veterans. The result is a breathtaking oil painting that measures 377 feet around and 42 feet high. Longer than a football field and as tall as a four-story building, Philippoteaux's Cyclorama plunges visitors into the fury of Pickett's Charge, when Confederate troops attacked Union forces on Cemetery Ridge—one of the fiercest and bloodiest battles of the Civil War.

Philippoteaux's Self-Portrait: Paul Philippoteaux painted himself into the *Battle of Gettysburg* Cyclorama. Just to the right of Philippoteaux is his self-portrait: an officer leaning against a tree with sword in hand.

Gettysburg in Boston: The Gettysburg Cyclorama was displayed at the Exhibition Hall in Boston in the 1880s. A poster from that time advertised the painting as a "sublime spectacle" that showed "glorious Gettysburg in all the awful splendor of real war."

CYCLORAMA HISTORY

The *Battle of Gettysburg* was first exhibited in Boston in 1884. There, some 200,000 visitors saw the painting. It remained in private hands—moving from various storage facilities and exhibition halls—until the government acquired it in the 1940s. For many years, its home was a tile-covered building on Baltimore Pike, which lacked temperature and humidity control. The painting deteriorated until the Cyclorama Center was completed in 1962 as part of the National Park Service's Mission 66 program, the largest program for park service improvements ever initiated. It was housed there for more than 40 years. In 2008, the Cyclorama was moved to the Gettysburg National Military Park Museum and Visitor Center.

> *There is nothing . . . better worth seeing.*
>
> —*The Watchman*, in a review of the Gettysburg Cyclorama exhibit, Boston, February 18, 1885

Over the years, the *Battle of Gettysburg* survived fires, leaks, tears, rotting, and display in hot, dusty halls. To squeeze into exhibition spaces, it was sliced into panels. More than 15 feet of its sky was cut away. By the late 1990s, parts of the painting were nearly beyond repair. Cracked paint over creased canvas and decades of dirt and grime covered much of the surface.

Flag: This souvenir touted the Cyclorama as the "grandest sight of this age," telling visitors, "you will come again and again."

Cyclorama Souvenir: This 1885 program from the Boston Cyclorama exhibit features both Union and Confederate soldiers.

Pickett's Charge: The *Battle of Gettysburg* Cyclorama captures the desperate fighting that occurred on July 3 during Pickett's Charge.

Saving the Cyclorama

Saving the Cyclorama demanded painstaking work by conservation specialists. The experts repaired unstable sections of the canvas and restored original details lost during previous conservation attempts. The conservation was a five-year, multimillion-dollar international effort, the largest of its kind ever undertaken on the continent.

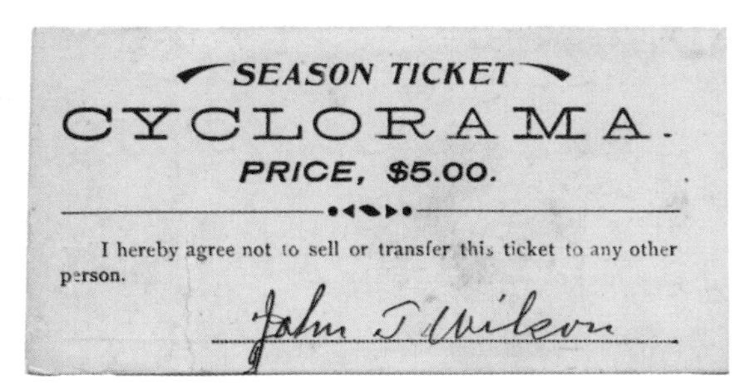

SEASON TICKET
CYCLORAMA.
PRICE, $5.00.

I hereby agree not to sell or transfer this ticket to any other person.

John T. Wilson

Season Ticket: This season ticket belonged to Confederate veteran John T. Wilson of Company H, 25th Virginia Infantry, who fought on Culp's Hill.

Now exhibited in its own unique viewing gallery, the *Battle of Gettysburg* includes a canopy that obscures the building's architectural features and a three-dimensional diorama with stone walls, broken fences, and shattered trees that carry the painted scene into the foreground. With these improvements, the Cyclorama can now be viewed the way Philippoteaux intended—as a powerful sight that brought many Civil War veterans to tears when it was first unveiled in Boston in 1884.

Battle Scene: A group of American entrepreneurs hired French artist Paul Philippoteaux to paint the *Battle of Gettysburg* Cyclorama. It took Philippoteaux and his team of assistants more than a year to complete it.

A New Birth of Freedom: The Civil War film *A New Birth of Freedom* is narrated by Academy Award-winning actor Morgan Freeman and educates visitors on the Battle of Gettysburg. After the film, visitors are led upstairs to the Cyclorama viewing platform.

Just a few short months after the Battle of Gettysburg, President Abraham Lincoln called for "a new birth of freedom" in his Gettysburg Address. Consequently, he redefined the future of the United States.

Today, visitors can learn more about the Battle of Gettysburg and the Civil War by seeing the film *A New Birth of Freedom* in the Museum and Visitor Center. Narrated by Morgan Freeman, the film also features the voices of Marcia Gay Harden and Sam Waterston. It is sponsored by the History Channel and shown in its own theater. A powerful documentary, *A New Birth of Freedom* sets the stage for the Gettysburg experience, placing the battle's monumental events into the larger context of American history—communicating that what happened in the past is very relevant today.

The Museum Experience

The four years of the American Civil War were the bloodiest in the nation's history. Some 620,000 soldiers and sailors died—a little less than 2 percent of the population. Today, a loss on the same scale would equal 6 million deaths. At Gettysburg alone, roughly 11,000 men died and another 40,000 were wounded, captured, or missing. These 51,000 casualties equaled about 20 times the population of the small Pennsylvania town.

Slave Shackles: Though the Civil War was first waged to preserve the Union, it increasingly became a battle for freedom.

Union Flag: The 34 stars on this 1861 flag include the 11 states of the Confederacy. Because the Union did not agree with the South's secession, it continued to represent the Southern states on its flag throughout the war.

Americans fought one another over three fundamental issues: the survival of the Union, the fate of slavery, and the common rights of citizenship. The war resolved the first two issues. The nation struggles with the third to this day.

I would strike down my own brother if he dare to raise a hand to destroy the flag.

— Private James Welsh, 78th Illinois Infantry, 1861

CAUSES OF WAR

After the American Revolution, the people of the United States invented a new nation, guided by the Constitution and personal beliefs about freedom and progress. They struggled, however, with the issue of slavery. Some considered it a mortal sin, others God's will, and still others a lifelong sentence to labor and oppression.

As the United States grew wealthier, more populous, and more powerful, these strains began to pull the nation apart. The Declaration of Independence and the U.S. Constitution inspired compromise, but both documents contained seeds of dissension. The Constitution had protections for slavery written into its text, since representatives from slave states had refused to sign the document without them. And the simple words from the Declaration, "All men are created equal," held different meanings for different Americans.

In 1830, Massachusetts Senator Daniel Webster urged his colleagues not to let these disagreements about rights and liberties jeopardize the nation, rallying Americans with his cry, "Liberty and Union!" But the conflict grew more pronounced—and more complex—over time. By 1850, the United States enslaved more people than any other country in the world. Economically, this human property was more valuable than the nation's railroads and factories combined.

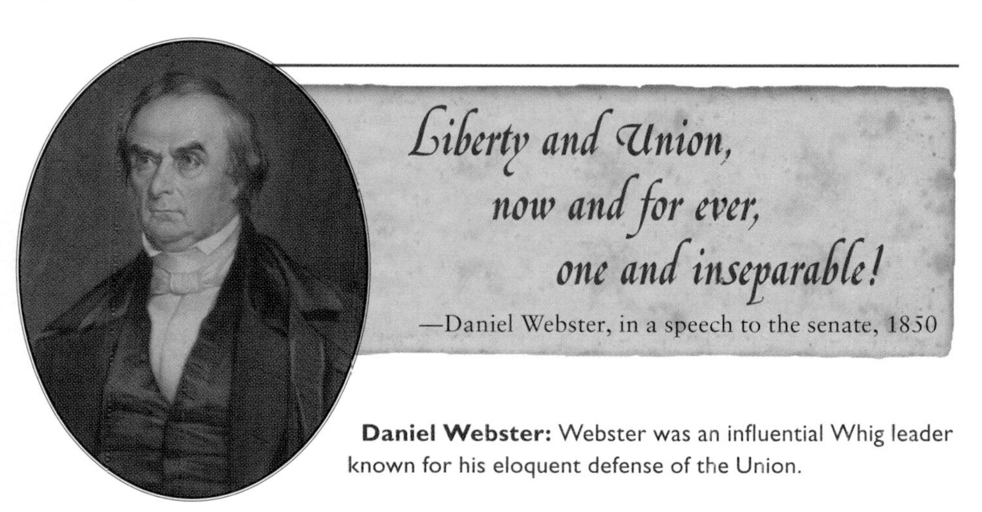

Daniel Webster: Webster was an influential Whig leader known for his eloquent defense of the Union.

The Civil War forced the American people to confront new questions: If a slave escapes to freedom, does he or she become an American? If a Southerner rebels against the government, does he or she remain an American? Who was an American in the 1800s?

Americans at War: The Union and Confederate armies each enlisted hundreds of thousands of men. The majority of Union soldiers came from New York (448,850), Pennsylvania (337,936), Illinois (259,092), and Indiana (196,363), while the Confederate troops were represented most strongly by Virginia (160,857), Tennessee (141,728), Georgia (135,774),

and Alabama (106,803). Only 12 states had enlistments on both sides, including Tennessee (51,225 Union, 141,728 Confederate), Louisiana (29,276 Union, 69,840 Confederate), and Kentucky (75,760 Union, 28,038 Confederate).

Slavery in the Territories

By 1860, the end of the United States was a looming possibility. Some Northern abolitionists preached, "No union with slaveholders." Other white Southerners believed they needed to create a new country to preserve their way of life and right to own slaves. In Kansas, Americans had already begun to murder one another over the issue of extending slavery into the territories.

These territories became a growing point of contention. Many white Southerners hoped for an empire of slavery that would include Cuba, much of Mexico, and stretch to the Pacific, but most Northerners opposed slavery in the western territories. They feared that small farmers without slaves would be unable to compete and survive. For decades, the battle over the westward expansion of slavery was mostly a war of words. But Americans kept moving west, and soon the debate turned bloody.

By the presidential election of 1860, the United States was deeply divided. Four men ran for president, which splintered the vote. Most Americans lived in Northern states, and the majority of voters there chose the Republican Party and Abraham Lincoln. The Republicans were determined to prevent the spread of slavery into the western territories. Largely for this, Lincoln—who wasn't even on the ballot in nine Southern states—was a menace in the eyes of many Southern slaveholders. In the end, however, Lincoln won about 40 percent of the popular vote and the presidency.

Territory Dispute: New York newspaper editor Horace Greeley helped compile this book for the 1860 election, which promised readers a thorough review of slavery in the territories.

The time for compromise has now passed, and the South is determined to maintain her position, and make all who oppose her smell Southern powder and taste Southern steel.

—Jefferson Davis, Inaugural Address, February 16, 1861

Southern Secession

On December 20, 1860, South Carolina declared its independence from the United States, formally stating that "the non-slaveholding States . . . have encouraged and assisted thousands of our slaves to leave their homes." Six other Southern states followed over the next few weeks; together, they formed the Confederate States of America. On February 8, 1861, before Abraham Lincoln had even taken office, the Confederacy adopted its own constitution. By March, these seven states had ratified a new constitution for the Confederate States of America and elected Jefferson Davis their first president. Meanwhile, other Southern states held conventions to decide the issue of secession. Southerners pointed to the Declaration of Independence for proof that the 13 original colonies were "free, sovereign, and independent states." The Constitution, they said, was a contract that any state could end. The U.S. government never recognized the right of the Southern states to leave the Union, though. Their stars remained on the American flag throughout the war.

The First Shot

The Civil War began at about 4:30 a.m. on April 12, 1861, when Confederate batteries opened on Fort Sumter—claimed by both the Confederate state of South Carolina and the U.S. government. About 85 federal troops waited anxiously inside Fort Sumter, including several men who would play important roles at Gettysburg. Abner Doubleday later wrote that he believed the first shot "seemed to bury itself in the masonry about a foot from my head, in very unpleasant proximity to my right ear."

Fort Sumter: Both the Confederate state of South Carolina and the Union claimed Fort Sumter, which guarded the entrance to the Charleston harbor. In 1861, President Lincoln decided to resupply Fort Sumter without bringing in weapons or troops—and Confederate President Jefferson Davis gave the order to take it.

Over the next two weeks, Fort Sumter fell, and President Lincoln called for 75,000 volunteers to suppress the rebellion. Virginia voted to secede, and Tennessee, Arkansas, and North Carolina followed, joining the seven states of the Deep South in the Confederate States of America.

Two Presidents

Abraham Lincoln and Jefferson Davis were both born in Kentucky—just one year and approximately 80 miles apart. Each man came to represent a different region of the country and a different way of life. And each became a president.

Abraham Lincoln and Mary Todd met in Springfield, Illinois, and married in 1842. She was from a prominent slaveholding family in Lexington, Kentucky; he was a self-made man. Abraham Lincoln worked as a grocer, postmaster, and surveyor, and studied law in his spare hours. He rose to fame as a lawyer, congressman, and candidate for the U.S. Senate. On March 4, 1861, he was inaugurated on the steps of the U.S. Capitol, two weeks after Jefferson Davis became president of the Confederate States of America.

Jefferson Davis had a long career of service to his country. He was a graduate of West Point, a U.S. congressman and senator from Mississippi, a hero of the Mexican War, and a secretary of war. When the South seceded, he was elected president of the Confederacy, though in his heart he had hoped for a military command.

Confederate Cabinet: A drawing of Confederate President Jefferson Davis and his cabinet. Davis called the day he resigned his seat in the U.S. Senate the saddest of his life.

Jefferson Davis had married 18-year-old Varina Howell in 1845 when he was 36—against her parents' wishes. Varina Davis helped her husband in his career, as a hostess and by editing his speeches and letters. But she called politics "everything which darkens the sunlight and contracts the happy sphere of home."

The excitement of war faded quickly as brutal, bloody combat swept across the nation. Civilians felt the horror of war at their doorsteps, particularly in the South. Eager recruits at the First Battle of Manassas—if they survived—became hardened veterans two years later.

Letters Home: Civil War soldiers often wrote about their hardships in letters home. "Oh, sister," wrote one Confederate soldier, "you folks at home can have no idea of what a soldier must endure."

Second Battle of Bull Run (Manassas): Union troops from the 41st New York Infantry in Manassas, Virginia, 1862. The Confederates won a solid victory at Manassas, bringing them to the height of their power.

To Abraham Lincoln, preserving the nation justified war. He thought that if a state could leave the Union, then the American experiment in democracy would be over. But Confederate President Jefferson Davis believed that he was leading a second American revolution—one that would create a new nation, preserve slavery, and defend Southern soil.

Military Objectives

The political goals of the Confederacy were to establish a new nation, preserve a way of life based on slave labor, and ensure the spread of slavery into new territories. The Confederacy also hoped to persuade foreign countries to recognize it as an independent nation and to draw bordering states into its new government. Militarily, the South aimed to defeat the Union army in a decisive victory and convince the United States to let the Confederacy go its own way, break any blockade of Southern ports, and turn back Union invasions of the South.

The United States' political goal at the start of the war was to bring the seceded states back into one nation. Unlike the South, the United States had to win the war—a draw would leave the country divided. Its military objectives were to defeat the Confederate army in a decisive victory and convince the Confederacy to give up the fight, blockade Southern ports to choke off cotton exports and imports of weapons and other goods from Europe, and conquer and occupy the South, an area twice the size of the original thirteen colonies.

71st New York Volunteers: Soldiers' comrades were often their neighbors, which created close friendships and painful losses. To keep up morale, they turned to music, poker, whiskey, religion, cards, and writing.

Volunteers Wanted: Few Confederate recruiting posters exist today. This one from 1861 attempted to fill the places of soldiers from the 2nd Virginia Infantry who died in the First Battle of Manassas.

In the Army Now

In the first weeks of the Civil War, both sides had more volunteers than they could train and equip. Thousands of men were turned away. But as hope for a brief war vanished, the armies looked for ways to enlist more soldiers and keep them longer. Both sides extended the terms of enlistment—in the North to three years and in the South for the duration of the war.

By 1862, volunteers were no longer enough. The Confederacy started a draft in April, and the United States followed the next year. Men with money could escape the draft by paying a fee or hiring a substitute. In the South, one white male was exempt from every plantation with 20 or more slaves.

The War at Home

Hundreds of thousands of families on both sides endured the death of loved ones, and many wives and children barely scraped by on their soldiers' wages. Yet Northerners and Southerners essentially lived through different wars. The economy and manufacturing of the North boomed, making the Union army the best equipped and supplied to that time, but the war devastated much of the South. Even victories were costly for the Confederacy, because most of the fighting swept across Southern fields and farms.

> *I cannot say we are eager for a fight, but as veterans of many pitched battles we are willing at least . . . to again give battle to our foes.*
>
> —Henry T. Lewis, 16th Mississippi Infantry, June 23, 1863

The Union navy also blockaded Southern ports. This created shortages and high prices in the South and made it difficult for the Confederate army to equip and supply its soldiers. Blockade runners like the *Georgiana* attempted to slip through the blockade to bring in goods and supplies. Some succeeded, but the *Georgiana*, with her cargo of buttons, pins, fabric and china, was run aground by the Union navy.

Army Revolver: Most cavalrymen preferred revolvers, such as this 1860 Colt.

First National Flag of the Confederacy, 1861: The first Confederate flag was called the Stars and Bars. In 1863, the design of the flag was changed to avoid confusion with the U.S. flag, especially on the battlefield. Patriotic slogans like these were unusual on national flags.

Union Infantrymen: Union soldiers, bolstered by the strong industry of the North, were generally better outfitted than Confederate troops. They were issued such items as a "bulls-eye" tin canteen, oval waistbelt plate, painted canvas haversack, Springfield rifle musket, socket bayonet, knapsack, and wool forage cap, left.

Confederate Infantrymen: Confederate soldiers received such items as a percussion cap box, Palmetto armory musket, socket bayonet, bayonet scabbard, slouch hat, cartridge box, and canteen, right. One Confederate soldier complained, "Reduced to the minimum, the private soldier consisted of one man, one hat, one jacket, one shirt, one pair of pants, one pair of drawers, one pair of shoes, and one pair of socks."

THE WAR ON SLAVERY

Abraham Lincoln and most Northerners went to war to preserve the Union, but for African Americans, the Civil War was about ending slavery. From the first shot, the chaos of war gave enslaved people a chance to escape to freedom. Wherever the army went, tens of thousands of fugitive slaves rushed to its lines. Many spent the war as servants to Union army units.

By 1863, Abraham Lincoln and the U.S. Army had come to see the logic of enlisting African American soldiers. Black volunteers brought desperately needed manpower into the army. And they were eager to fight, manning Union supply lines, building fortifications, and ultimately taking up arms for their own freedom—hoping that their courage under fire might prove all African Americans worthy of equality and full citizenship at the war's end.

U.S. Colored Troops: A group of African American soldiers rest in Aiken's Landing, Virginia. For most of the war, only white officers were permitted to lead U.S. Colored Troops. African American officers—such as Martin L. Delaney, the first black major—were rare.

African American troops who volunteered for the army were designated United States Colored Troops. They marched into combat, fighting bravely on such battlefields as Port Hudson, Louisiana; Fort Wagner, South Carolina; and Petersburg, Virginia. By the war's end, the army had roughly 164 regiments of USCT infantry, artillery, and cavalry. In all, some 200,000 black soldiers and sailors served their country in uniform.

The Emancipation Proclamation

With the Emancipation Proclamation, Abraham Lincoln freed all enslaved people in the Southern states that were in rebellion against the United States. Slaveholders in the South saw the proclamation as a call for a slave rebellion. The act encouraged slaves to flee to Union lines and join the Union army—and it took away thousands of African Americans who had been laboring for the Confederate war effort.

Emancipation Proclamation: An artistic rendering of the Emancipation Proclamation, signed by President Lincoln on January 1, 1863. The proclamation declared that "all persons held as slaves" in the seceded states were free.

The Emancipation Proclamation still left tens of thousands enslaved in Missouri, Kentucky, Maryland, and Delaware, though. Lincoln believed he lacked the legal authority to free slaves in any state that remained in the Union, and he was unwilling to risk losing any of these border states to the Confederacy.

Abraham Lincoln agonized over the Emancipation Proclamation—its wording, when he should release it, and what the country's reaction would be. As president, he believed he could not legally end slavery. But in wartime, his power and responsibilities as commander-in-chief led him to do what he believed to be right. "I never, in my life," he said, "felt more certain that I was doing right than I do in signing this paper."

> *Let the white fight for what the[y] want and we Negroes fight for what we want . . . Liberty must take the day and nothing shorter.*
>
> —African American soldier, U.S. Colored Troops, Louisiana

Lincoln's Cabinet: The first reading of the Emancipation Proclamation occurred before President Lincoln's cabinet on July 22, 1862. The proclamation was finally issued on January 1, 1863.

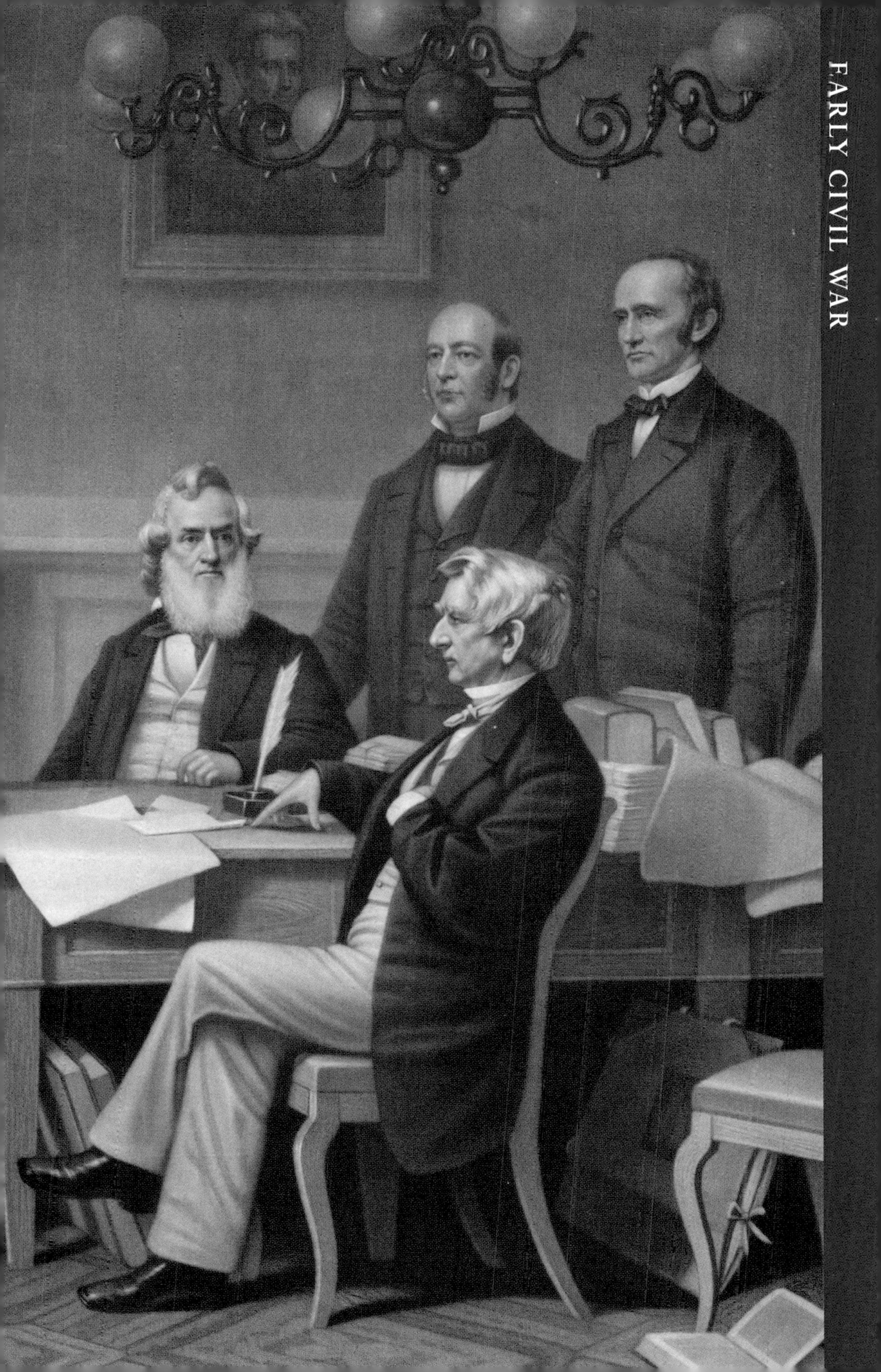

General Robert E. Lee and his army had already inflicted four demoralizing losses on the Union army in 12 months. The Battle of Chancellorsville in May had been Lee's most daring victory. However, Chancellorsville had cost Lee nearly one quarter of his army, including his ablest commander, General Thomas "Stonewall" Jackson. It also left Lee's army starved for supplies.

There is no better way of defending a long line than by moving into the enemy's territory.

—Robert E. Lee, March 1863

Robert E. Lee: General Lee was a dynamic, thoughtful leader. "There never were such men in an army before," Lee said of his troops. "They will go anywhere and do anything if properly led."

General Lee believed his best hope lay in a bold gamble—an invasion of Pennsylvania. He took a great risk in leading his army north. Some of his officers were commanding a corps or division for the first time. Yet Lee knew that a Confederate victory in Pennsylvania might damage Northern morale, erode support for the war, and disrupt Union plans for the summer. He also knew that moving the struggle north would give Southern farmers a chance to plant and harvest. Pennsylvania's fields and barns would supply the Army of Northern Virginia, and the army could send crops and livestock south.

On June 3, 1863, the Confederate army began to move. Using the Blue Ridge Mountains to screen its movement, it marched toward Maryland and crossed the Potomac River. For two weeks, the Confederates occupied towns across south-central Pennsylvania, gathering food, shoes, horses, cattle, and other goods wherever they passed, and probing for the Union army. They liberated Winchester, Virginia, from a garrison of Union troops and took thousands of prisoners. They kidnapped hundreds of African Americans and sent them South into slavery.

As the Army of Northern Virginia drew near, the people of Harrisburg dug trenches to defend the state capital. On June 12, Pennsylvania Governor Andrew Curtin issued a proclamation calling for citizens to fill the ranks of the militia and defend their homes.

In late June, the Union Army of the Potomac marched north through Maryland in pursuit of the Army of Northern Virginia. The army crossed the Potomac, taking several roads north through Maryland to speed the advance.

The Size of an Army

Assembling an army was difficult enough, with thousands of men organized into various brigades, divisions, and corps. Moving it was harder still. Leading an army on a long march required good generalship and reliable tools. Accurate maps were crucial to getting tens of thousands of men to the right place at the right time along different roads and across unfamiliar ground.

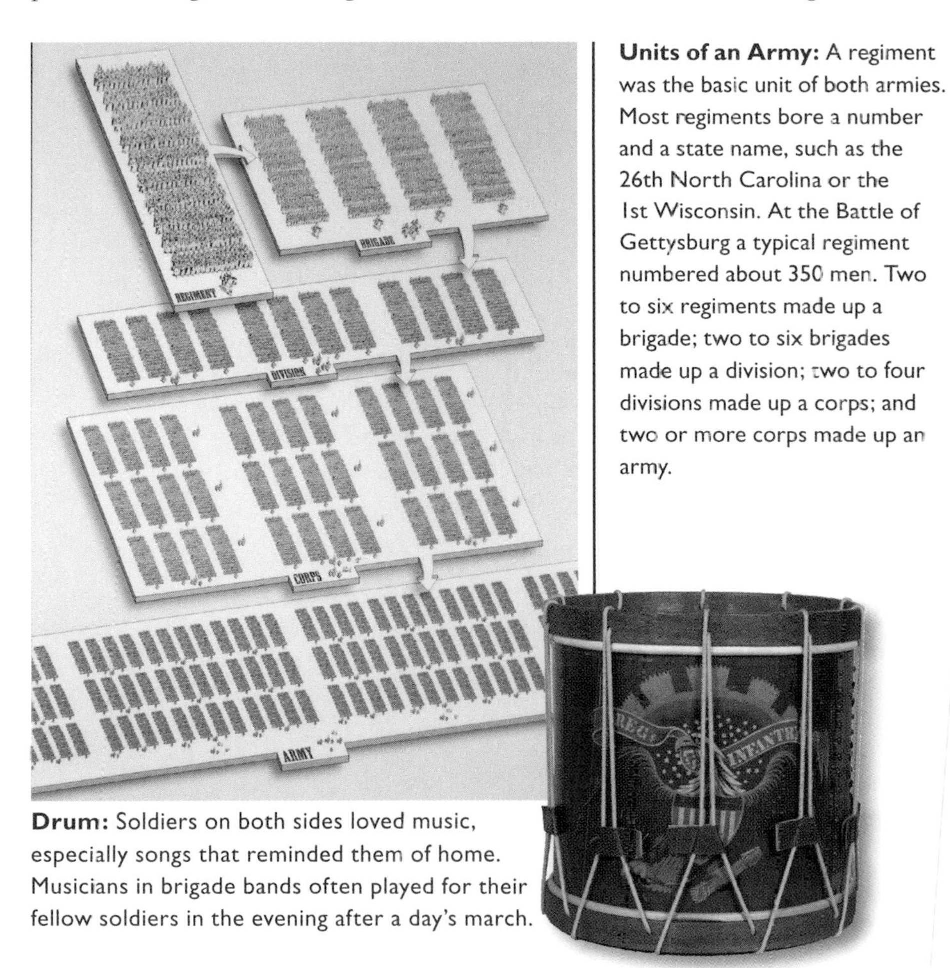

Units of an Army: A regiment was the basic unit of both armies. Most regiments bore a number and a state name, such as the 26th North Carolina or the 1st Wisconsin. At the Battle of Gettysburg a typical regiment numbered about 350 men. Two to six regiments made up a brigade; two to six brigades made up a division; two to four divisions made up a corps; and two or more corps made up an army.

Drum: Soldiers on both sides loved music, especially songs that reminded them of home. Musicians in brigade bands often played for their fellow soldiers in the evening after a day's march.

The Army of Northern Virginia was divided into three corps and had 75,000 men on the campaign to Pennsylvania. When it headed north, its wagon trains stretched for 60 miles. The Army of the Potomac, in seven corps, included some 90,000 men. Alone, the Union army would have made up the 10th largest city in the United States—larger than any city in the South except New Orleans.

A Day on the Campaign

From a soldier's point of view, a campaign was exhausting, frustrating, boring, and unpredictable. Unlike officers, whose baggage was carted in wagons, enlisted men had to carry all of their belongings on their backs. On long marches, they were unwilling to carry more than the absolute essentials. Even so, infantrymen ended up carrying about 30 to 40 pounds.

Flesh and blood cannot sustain such heat and fatigue . . . . I have seen men dropping, gasping, dying, or already dead.

—Randolph Shotwell, 8th Virginia Infantry Regiment, June 17, 1863

Soldiers were ordered to march in driving rain and baking heat. They might walk two miles a day or 25. A march often started as early as 2:00 a.m., as soldiers were roused out of their blankets with bugles, drums, and shouts. They got up, packed their gear, and ate breakfast. Then they waited for orders, sometimes all day. A bad map, news about the enemy, or confusing orders could send a column back and forth over the same ground.

Haversack: Civil War soldiers used haversacks like this one to carry the bare essentials during a march.

The armies usually halted once every hour for about 10 minutes each time, but in emergencies, units on both sides marched nearly to exhaustion. Those weakened by disease or fatigue dropped out of line and lay by the roadside. Many rested and rejoined their units; others died by the road or were picked up by ambulances.

Sleeping Quarters: Officers' quarters were much nicer than those of enlisted men. Officers generally slept in wall tents like the one at right, and they provided their own gear. Each junior officer was allowed one trunk that was carried in one of the baggage wagons. Higher-ranking officers were allowed more baggage.

Soldiers on campaign usually stopped around midday and cooked a meal. For Union soldiers, a day's rations were a pound of hardtack, three-fourths of a pound of salt pork, and a little sugar, coffee, and salt. Confederates' rations were skimpier, but they ate well on the Gettysburg campaign, thanks to the farms and stores of Maryland and Pennsylvania. A good end to a day's march was dry weather, time to forage for food, and wood to cook supper. On the road to Gettysburg, though, the last march for many units ended with a sprint toward the sound of cannon fire and a headlong rush into battle.

Clashing Cavalry

As the armies moved north toward Pennsylvania, Confederate and Union cavalry units rode between the two armies, clashing almost continuously. In the first three weeks of June 1863, some 2,500 cavalry troopers were killed, wounded, captured, or missing.

Confederate cavalry outrode, outfought, or outgeneraled the Union horsemen during much of the early war. But at Brandy Station in early June, the Union cavalry attacked without warning, slugged it out through repeated counterattacks, and withdrew in good order. Some 20,000 men were involved on both sides during the 16-hour fight. It was the largest cavalry battle of the Civil War.

The Rebels Are Coming

Confederate troopers rode into the Gettysburg town square about 3:00 p.m. on June 26—"cursing, brandishing their revolvers, and firing right and left," wrote local girl Tillie Pierce. One soldier led away her favorite horse. Other soldiers helped themselves to horses, feed, hats, shoes, candy, whiskey, blankets, and other goods. At A. D. Buehler's drugstore, they reportedly left Confederate bills in payment.

As I stood there begging and weeping, I was so shocked and insulted, I shall never forget it.

—Gettysburg citizen Tillie Pierce, on how the Confederates took her horse

Soldier and Horse: A Civil War–era drawing of a soldier and his horse.

The people of Gettysburg had known the "rebels" were coming. To prepare, they had shipped away money in the town bank, sent a railroad car full of goods to Philadelphia, and hid their valuables and livestock. Many of the townspeople also fled—especially the men, who were leading their family's most vital possession, their horses, to safety.

Black Pennsylvanians were particularly vulnerable. Fugitive slaves were in constant danger of being arrested and returned to slaveholders, and even free blacks could be kidnapped and sold in the South. Nearly 200 free African Americans lived in and around Gettysburg in June 1863. By the time Confederate troops appeared, most had escaped.

Town of Gettysburg: Pictured is the northern portion of Gettysburg, located near the Lutheran Theological Seminary. Gettysburg citizen Harriet Bayly said before the battle, "The whole air seemed charged with conditions which go before a storm; everybody anxious, neighbor asking neighbor what was going to happen."

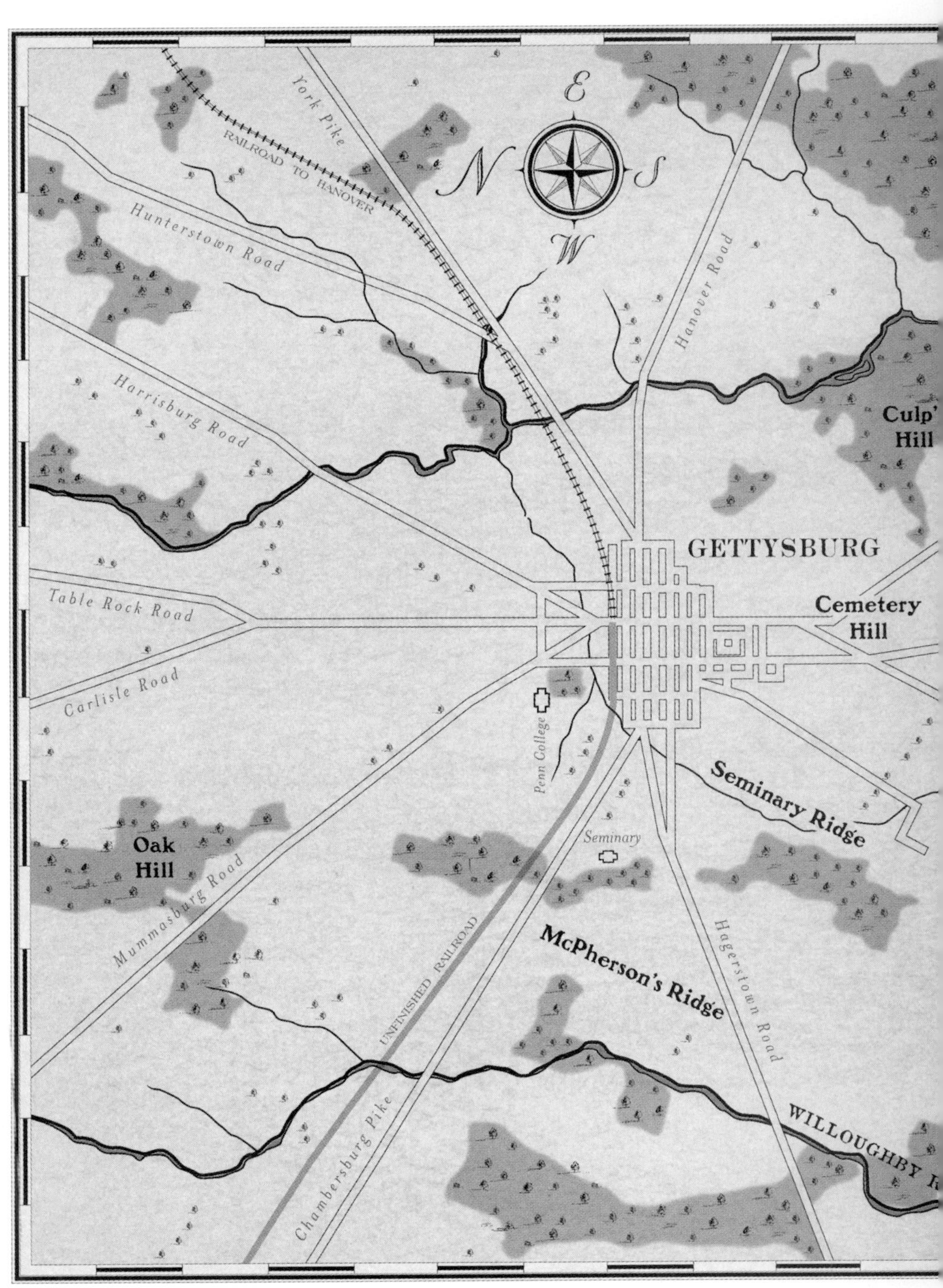

Battlefield of Gettysburg: A rendering of the town and surrounding area of Gettysburg in 1863.

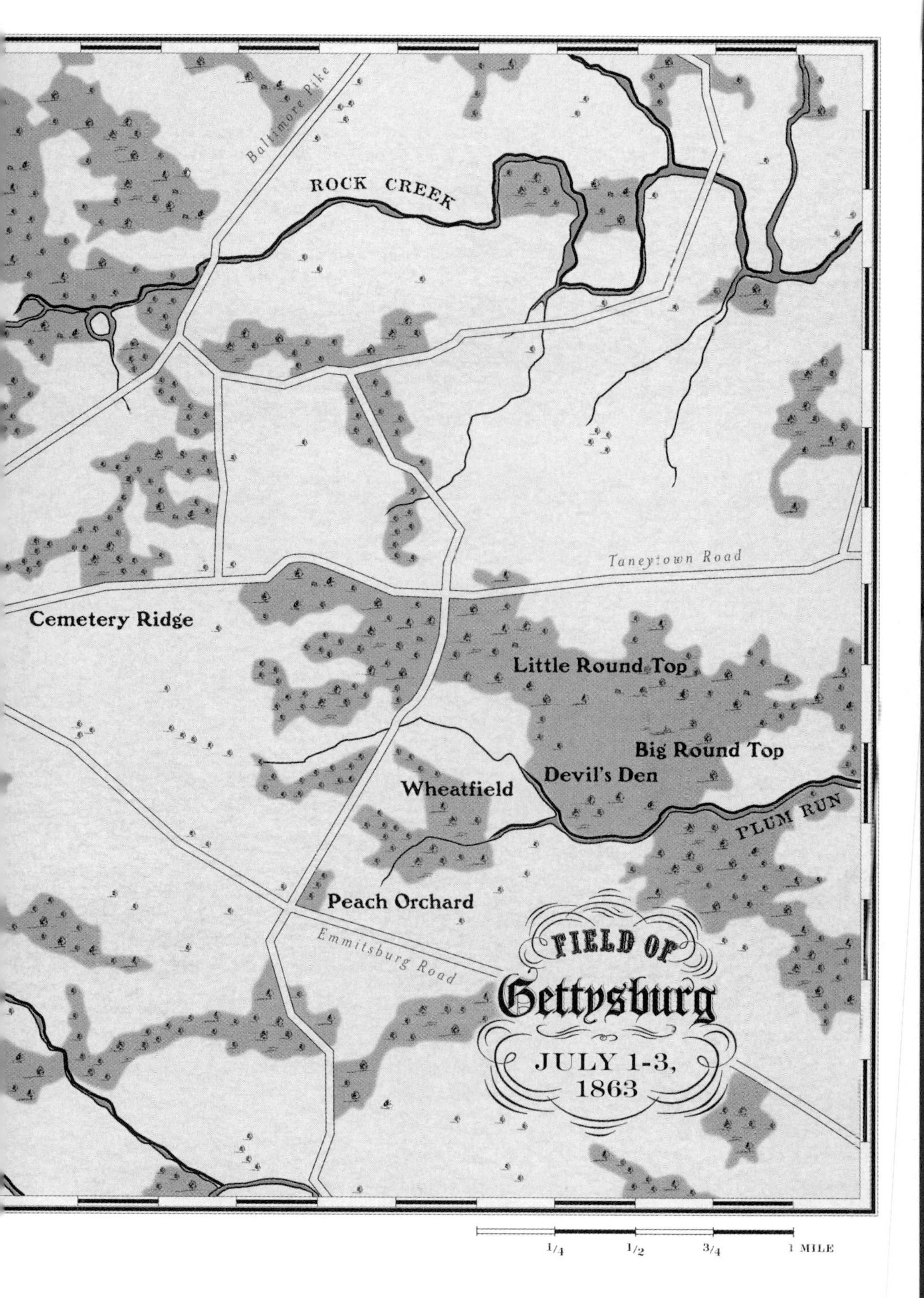
Baltimore Pike
ROCK CREEK
Taneytown Road
Cemetery Ridge
Little Round Top
Big Round Top
Devil's Den
Wheatfield
PLUM RUN
Peach Orchard
Emmitsburg Road
FIELD OF
Gettysburg
JULY 1-3,
1863
1/4
1/2
3/4
1 MILE

The Army of Northern Virginia was spread out west, north, and east of Gettysburg on June 30, 1863. The Army of the Potomac was south and southeast. Ten roads converged at the town like the spokes of a wheel, drawing both armies in. It was just a matter of time before the two armies collided—the only question was where.

Each commander had the same hope: to gather his army before his opponent could do the same. The first army at full strength might have the chance to attack a smaller portion of the enemy's forces and destroy them. Union General George Meade knew the rough location of nearly 50,000 Confederates west of Gettysburg and had reports of other units east in York. Robert E. Lee, however, had no news from his cavalry. He believed the Union forces were still near Middleburg, Maryland, some 15 miles south of the Pennsylvania border.

Field Glasses: Signalmen used field glasses to monitor enemy activity and scout terrain. Union signalman Aaron Jerome might have been the first to see the Confederates advance. He was stationed in the cupola of the Lutheran Seminary the morning of July 1, 1863.

Lutheran Theological Seminary: From the cupola atop the Lutheran Seminary, Union General John Buford also watched the Confederates advance. For the Confederates, the same building was a landmark and a goal.

Day 1–July 1–7:30 a.m.

The First Shot

At dawn on July 1, 1863, neither George Meade nor Robert E. Lee was looking for a battle at Gettysburg. The biggest battle of the Civil War took both commanders by surprise.

> *Wednesday, July 1. A little after 7:00, the enemies advance . . . I took aim at an officer on a white or light gray horse and fired.*
>
> —Lieutenant Marcellus Jones, 8th Illinois Cavalry

Early that morning, General Henry Heth led a column of 7,000 Confederate soldiers toward Gettysburg on Chambersburg Pike. He saw the Union cavalrymen, but had orders from General Lee not to bring on a sustained fight.

Three miles west of Gettysburg, Union scout Lieutenant Marcellus Jones of the 8th Illinois Cavalry spotted the column of Confederate infantry. He sent a rider back with word that the Confederates were on their way. Then he borrowed a carbine from his sergeant, rested it on a rail fence, and fired a warning shot.

Heth's men responded with shots of their own and continued their march toward Gettysburg. Meanwhile, Union General John Buford led his 2,700 cavalrymen toward the McPherson farm one half mile west of Gettysburg and positioned them in an arc stretching from the west to the northeast, from Hagerstown to Harrisburg roads. The Battle of Gettysburg had begun.

First Shot: Erected in 1886, this marker honors Union Lieutenant Marcellus Jones, who fired the first shot at Gettysburg.

DAY 1–JULY 1–10:00 A.M. TO 2:00 P.M.

ON MCPHERSON'S RIDGE

The outnumbered Union cavalry of General John Buford fought through the morning to slow the Confederate advance. They dismounted, formed a line, fired until the Confederates got too close, and then pulled back to form again. One of the first Union infantry units to reach the battlefield and relieve General Buford's cavalry was the 1st Corps. One of its units, known as the Iron Brigade, rushed into battle on McPherson's Ridge and attacked the Confederates along a tiny stream called Willoughby Run.

In a grim and bloody hour-long battle, the 1st Corps defeated Heth's infantrymen and drove them back. After a lull, the Confederates attacked again. Both sides suffered heavy losses, but the Confederates managed to push the 1st Corps back.

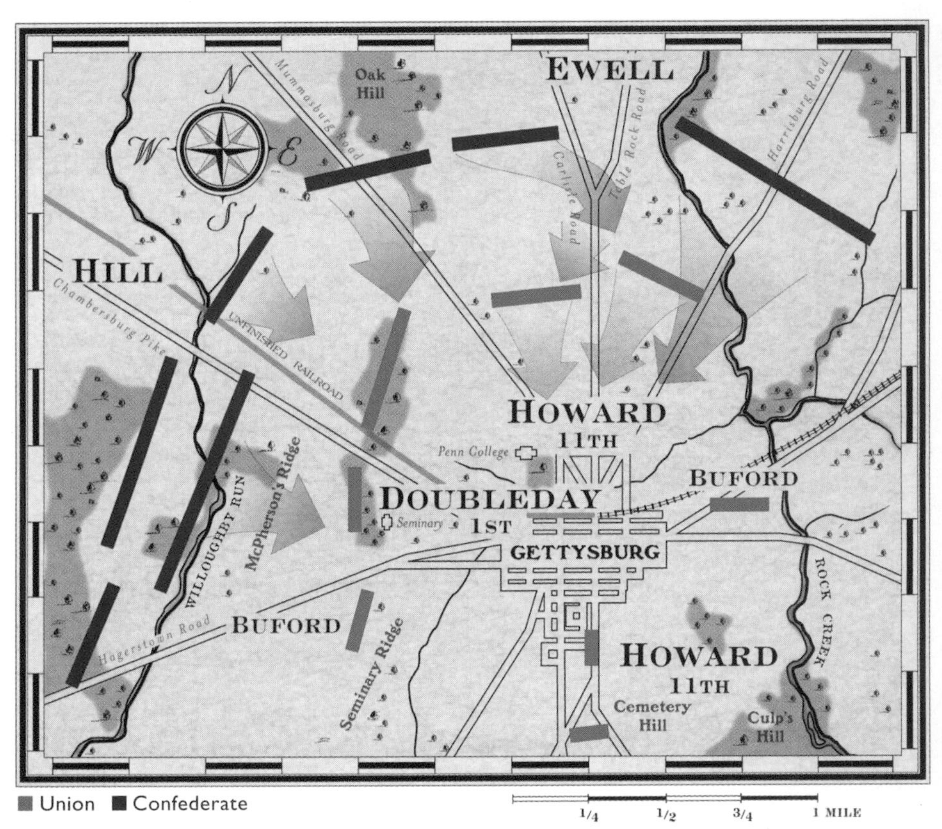

■ Union ■ Confederate

1/4 1/2 3/4 1 MILE

Day One: The first day of fighting took place close to the town, much of it centered on McPherson's Ridge. The Confederates eventually forced the Union army to retreat through the streets of Gettysburg and regroup on Cemetery Hill and Culp's Hill.

Day 1–July 1–3:00 p.m.

Collapse

By 3:00 p.m., the Confederates were attacking along a broad front north and west of town. On the Union right, some units held their ground and mounted a steady defense. But more retreated, and many began to run. Union General Oliver Howard's 11th Corps finally gave way.

By 4:00 p.m., the entire Union line had collapsed, and the Army of Northern Virginia marched into Gettysburg. The Union 1st and 11th Corps retreated south and east through the streets of Gettysburg to the hills behind town, having lost nearly 9,000 men in the day's fighting.

Artillery Sword: Short artillery swords, such as this one from 1861, were intended to serve as defensive weapons but proved impractical.

Cemetery Hill: The Union 1st and 11th Corps rallied on Cemetery Hill after their defeat north and west of Gettysburg.

DAY 1–JULY 1–EVENING

A DESPERATE DAY

At the end of the first day's fighting, some 3,000 men lay dead in the fields around Gettysburg. Roughly 13,000 were wounded or captured. Robert E. Lee's army had once again driven back the Army of the Potomac, as it had in battle after battle over the past year. Many Confederates were confident that the next day would see a crushing defeat of Meade's army.

Evergreen Cemetery Gatehouse on Cemetery Hill: After the fighting on July 1, Union soldiers halted their retreat from the Confederates in this area of Cemetery Hill.

The war had erupted in Gettysburg. Fighting swept through the streets of town as the Union 1st and 11th Corps retreated to Cemetery Hill with the Confederates in pursuit. Bullets whined through the air, and artillery fired down streets. The wounded sought aid and shelter in private homes and public buildings. By late afternoon, the town was behind Confederate lines.

DAY 2–JULY 2–10:00 A.M.

LEE'S DILEMMA

On the morning of July 2, General Robert E. Lee remained unsure how much of the Union army he faced. He had no information from his cavalry about the enemy's position—General J. E. B. Stuart and his troopers were still missing. Lee sent one of the staff officers to scout the left end of the Union line. Captain Samuel R. Johnston reported back that the Round Tops were unoccupied and the Union line was vulnerable on that flank.

Lee's infantry commanders, generals James Longstreet, A. P. Hill, and Richard Ewell, commanded the three corps of the Confederate army. None was eager to fight. Many of Hill's troops were exhausted from the first day's battle. Ewell didn't think his corps could take Cemetery Hill and Culp's Hill, and Longstreet urged Lee to move his entire army to better ground. But Lee ordered assaults on both ends of the Union line.

Setting these attacks in motion took nearly six hours. The position of the Union army had begun to take the shape of an upside-down fishhook with its barb on the east side of Culp's Hill and the long shank along Cemetery Ridge. The Confederate army stretched in a longer, similar line to the north and west of the Union position.

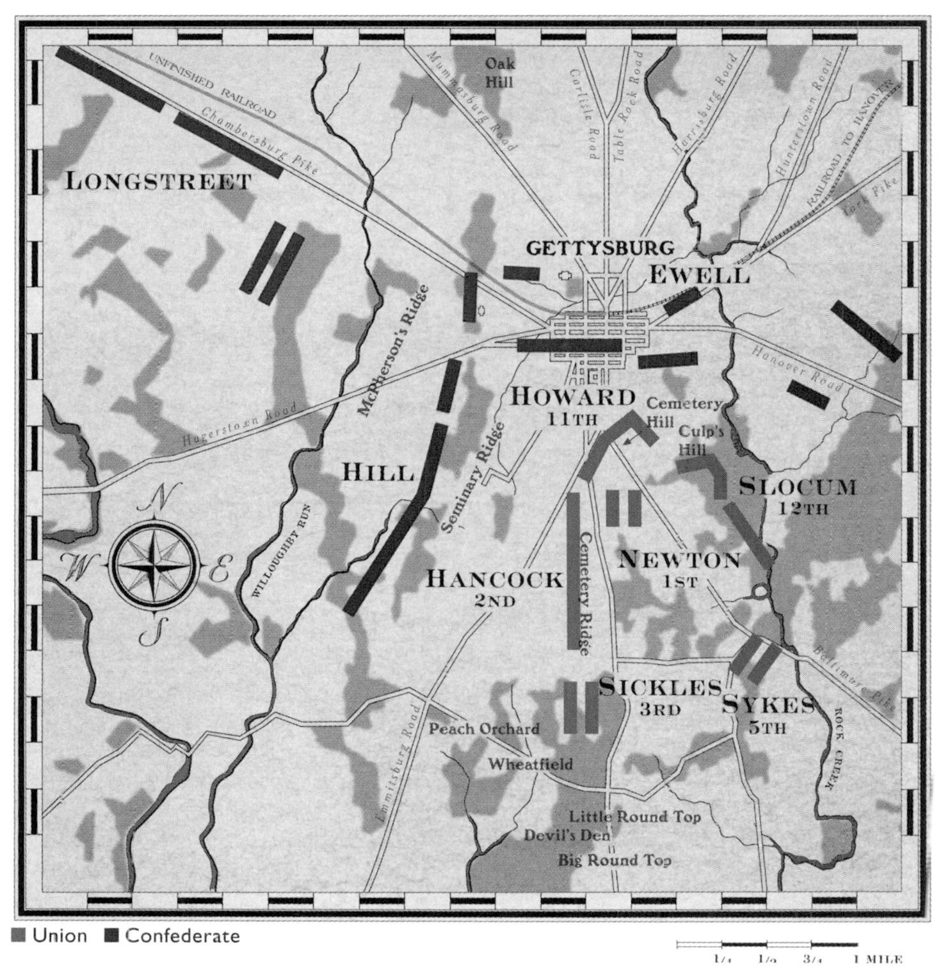

Day Two: The Union army took the form of a fishhook on the second day, stretching out along Cemetery Ridge and arching toward Culp's Hill. The Confederates took a similar position, mirroring the Union army in order to launch attacks on both ends of the enemy's line.

DAY 2–JULY 2–2:00 P.M.

CEMETERY RIDGE

Union General Daniel Sickles was the Army of the Potomac's most controversial general. A politician before the war, he was brave and reckless. Stationed on the left of the Union army, he didn't like his assigned position. Sickles saw higher ground along Emmitsburg Road, about a half mile ahead. About 2:00 p.m., ignoring his orders, he pushed his 3rd Corps forward.

Some of his troops occupied slightly higher ground at the Wheatfield and Peach Orchard, while others found good cover in Devil's Den. But the new line was longer, thinner, and more exposed. An hour later, General Meade rode up, furious that Sickles had disobeyed him. Shells began to explode around them, and Sickles offered to pull his troops back. "I wish to God you could," Meade responded, "but the enemy won't let you."

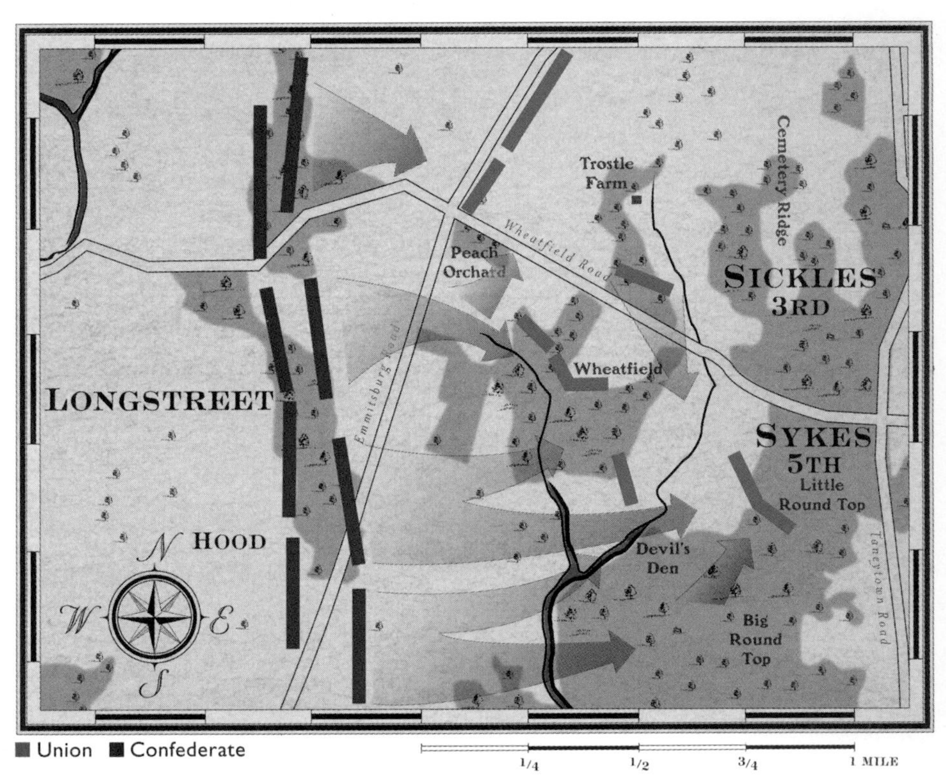

Day Two: Some of the fiercest fighting on the second day took place at the Wheatfield and Devil's Den, where Union General Dan Sickles moved his 3rd Corps against General Meade's orders. Confederate General John Hood charged into Devil's Den, and Union troops eventually gave way.

Day 2–July 2–4:00 p.m.

Devil's Den

Just after 4:00 p.m., Confederate General John B. Hood's division attacked Sickles's left flank at Little Round Top and around Devil's Den. Early in the action, a Union shell shattered one of Hood's arms, removing him from the battle. Fierce fighting ensued as Union troops stubbornly resisted the Confederate forces.

Firearm: This popular .577-caliber 1853 Enfield Rifle-Musket was manufactured in the United Kingdom. Both the North and South used foreign imports, although the Confederate troops relied more heavily on them.

Devil's Den: A dead Confederate soldier lies slumped among the massive boulders of Devil's Den. Southerners in particular were awestruck by the rugged nature of the Den, one calling the area a "wild, rocky labyrinth" with "weird, uncanny features."

Leaping over my prostrate line, I shouted the order, "Forward!" and started for the rocks. The response was a bound, a yell, and a rush . . .

—Colonel William F. Perry, 44th Alabama Infantry, Devil's Den

THE ROLE OF ARTILLERY

The main role of artillery was to support the infantry. During an infantry charge, gunners poured fire into the enemy's ranks to break up the assault. Artillery batteries also bombarded enemy positions before an attack, and gunners from both sides tried to disable their foes' artillery. Artillery brigades were divided into batteries, which usually included four to six cannon. Roughly 100 soldiers manned the guns, and hauling a battery's guns and ammunition required nearly as many horses.

Horse-drawn Artillery: Civil War batteries required extensive horse—and man—power. Artillerymen took care of the horses, guns, and gun carriages as part of their daily duties.

Napoleon Cannon: Napoleon cannon were widely used during the Civil War.

Some of the most common artillery pieces of the war were Napoleon cannon. Effective at up to three-quarters of a mile, they fired solid shot, exploding shells, or canister. On the move, the cannon were hooked to a limber—an ammunition chest on wheels—pulled by a team of six horses. During combat, the chests were kept a safe distance back, if possible, and the soldier designated "No. 5" carried the powder and shell to the gun. The Table of Fire glued inside the lid instructed gunners on the correct gun elevations for hitting targets at various distances.

Three corps opened the fight at 3:00.
They got drove back at 5:00.
Our regiment went into the fight
[after] 5:00 . . . Lost 223 out of 300.

—S. E. Martin, 1st Minnesota Infantry, July 2, 1863

Day 2–July 2–4:00 to 6:00 p.m.

Little Round Top

Little Round Top stood high and relatively open on the extreme end of the Union line. Whichever side held it could see much of the southern end of the battlefield. From the signalmen's post on Little Round Top, Union General Gouverneur K. Warren—sometimes called the savior of Gettysburg—saw Confederate General James Longstreet's corps massing for an attack. He hurried Union troops to defend the hill.

Little Round Top: This July 1863 photograph shows the Union breastworks—temporary fortifications of earth and wood—that were built on Little Round Top.

Just minutes before Longstreet's Confederates rushed up the rocky slope, Union Colonel Strong Vincent led his brigade across the top of the hill and a few paces down the other side. Vincent, Union Colonel Patrick O'Rorke, and Union Brigadier General Stephen Weed were mortally wounded in the fighting. Desperate fighting by the 20th Maine Infantry, led by Colonel Joshua Chamberlain, bolstered the left flank of the brigade. Chamberlain and his infantry were nearly driven back by Confederate Colonel William Oates, but they held in the end. Last-minute reinforcements—the 140th New York Infantry—helped rescue the right flank on the hill. Together, the five regiments saved Little Round Top for the Army of the Potomac.

Day 2–July 2–6:30 p.m.

Trostle Farm

At the end of the afternoon, Union troops in the Wheatfield and Peach Orchard gave way. One of the last batteries to pull back was the 9th Massachusetts. On the retreat, they were ordered to hold their position near the Trostle farm at all costs.

Union Buckle: Belt buckles like this were later found around Gettysburg.

Trostle Farm: Dead artillery horses lie scattered across the yard at the Trostle farm. A Confederate soldier recalled the fire of the 9th Massachusetts Battery, saying, "The terrible missiles of death were flying thick and fast everywhere."

The farm of Abraham and Catherine Trostle stood about halfway between Emmitsburg Road and Cemetery Ridge, directly in the path of the advancing Confederates. For 30 minutes, the 9th Massachusetts' battery held off Confederate infantry approaching from three sides—long enough for Union forces to form a line of battle along Cemetery Ridge. When they at last fell back, it came at the cost of one-quarter of their men, more than half their horses, and four cannon.

Day 2–July 2–6:00 to 7:00 p.m.

Charge of the 1st Minnesota

By late in the afternoon of July 2, Longstreet's attack had driven back Sickles's 3rd Corps and was threatening to break open the Union line. Union General Winfield Hancock saw a Confederate brigade advancing unchecked toward Cemetery Ridge. He found only one regiment on hand to stand in their way—the 1st Minnesota Infantry. "Do you see those colors?" he asked the regiment's commander, pointing toward the Confederates. Colonel William Colvill said he did. "Then take them," Hancock replied. Led by Colvill, 262 men of the 1st Minnesota Infantry charged into General Cadmus Wilcox's brigade of Alabamians, 1,600 men strong. Only 47 Minnesotans returned to Union lines. Although the Union losses were devastating, the charge of the 1st Minnesota bought precious time for Union reinforcements to arrive and hold the line.

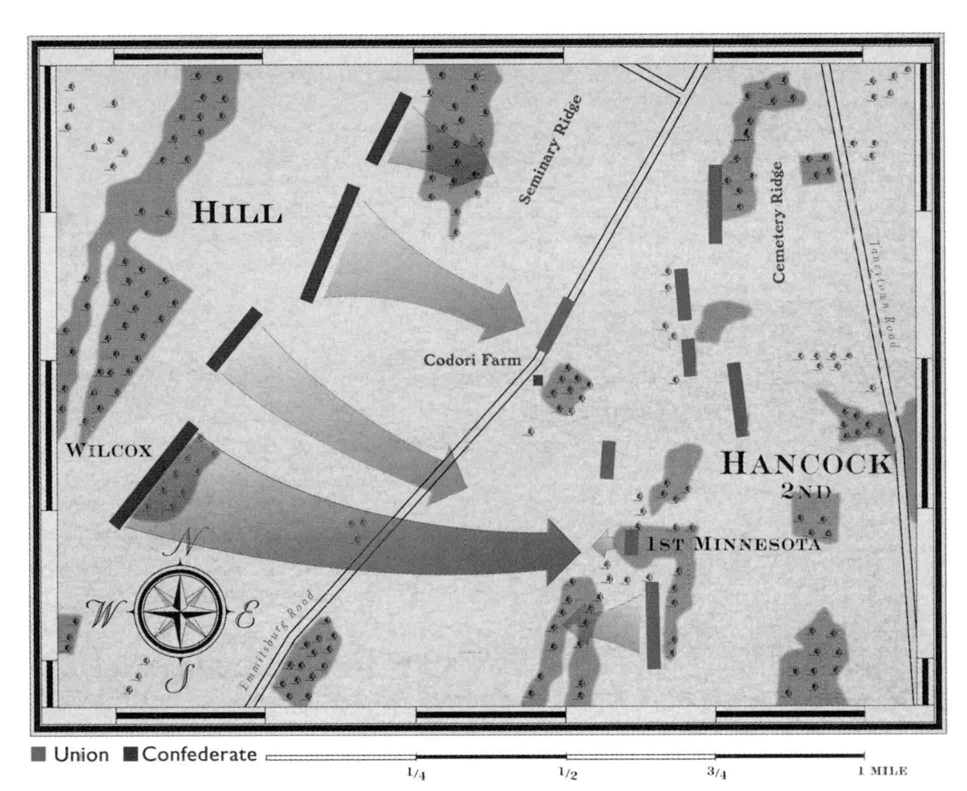

Day Two: Late in the afternoon on July 2, 1863, Confederate General A. P. Hill led an attack on Union troops along Cemetery Ridge. Despite being heavily outnumbered, the Union's 1st Minnesota Infantry charged Confederate General Cadmus Wilcox's brigade—losing more than three-quarters of its men.

Day 2–July 2–7:30 p.m.

On Cemetery Ridge

At dusk, part of Confederate General Ambrose Wright's brigade crossed Emmitsburg Road and swept past the Codori farm. The Georgians routed two Union regiments, captured a battery of guns, and rushed toward the crest of Cemetery Ridge.

There, they found themselves alone, with Union reinforcements approaching on three sides. The Confederates were forced to pull back. Wright reported that with a little support he could have held his ground—a conviction he would maintain to the end of his days.

Day 2–July 2–7:30 p.m.

On Two Hills

Confederate General Richard Ewell had orders from General Lee to demonstrate against the right flank of the Union army when he heard the sound of Longstreet's guns on the left. If the opportunity presented, Ewell had the discretion to escalate the demonstration into a full-scale attack.

General Richard S. Ewell: On July 2, Lee directed General Ewell to attack the right flank of the Union army on Culp's Hill. His artillery assault began in the late afternoon, but his infantry was delayed by Union fire from Cemetery Hill.

Culp's Hill: Throughout the second day of battle, gunfire zigzagged through the woods on Culp's Hill, riddling nearly all the trees in range with bullets. Union Captain George Thayer called it a "terrific crash of musketry."

As daylight faded, Ewell launched attacks first on Culp's Hill, then Cemetery Hill just south of Gettysburg. The soldiers fought until nearly 10:00 p.m., finding one another by the flash of their guns. Cannon and rifle fire tore through the branches and trunks of trees on both hills, riddling the landscape with bullets. The Confederates were repulsed on Cemetery Hill and gained a foothold on Culp's Hill, but no more.

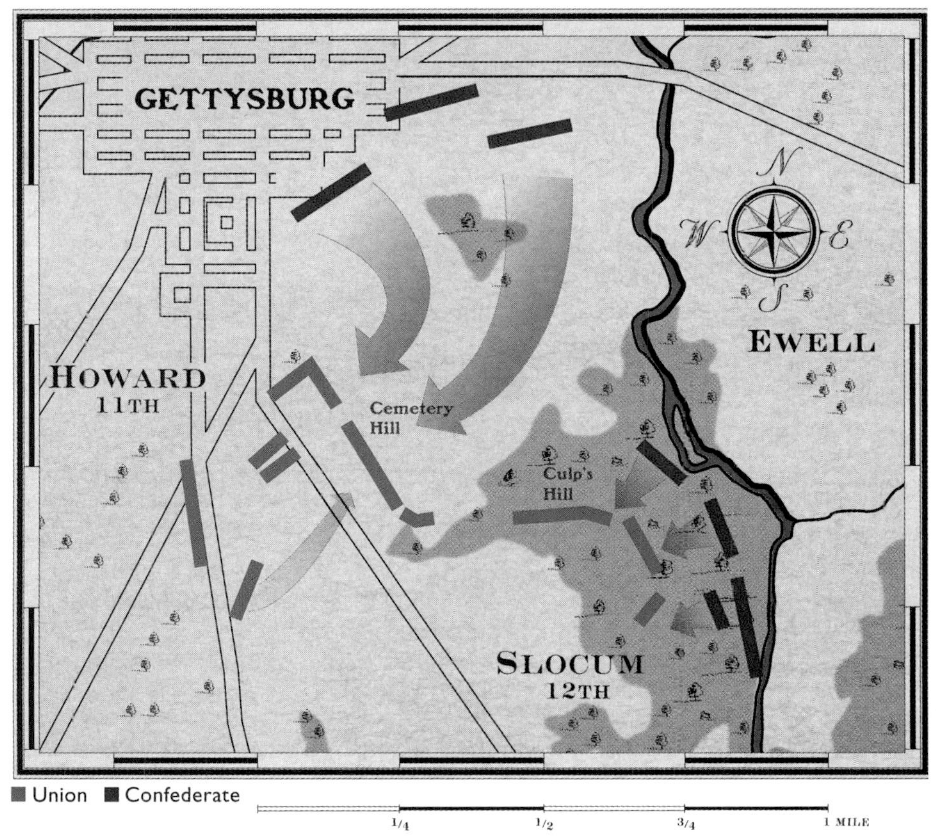

Day Two: On the evening of the second day, Confederate General Richard Ewell attacked the Union's 11th and 12th Corps on Cemetery Hill and Culp's Hill. The fighting continued through the night as the 12th Corps used breastworks to take shelter from the barrage of bullets.

THE ROLE OF INFANTRY

The clash of infantry decided nearly every major battle in the Civil War. The infantry's role was simple but bloody—to drive back the enemy and to take and hold ground. An infantry assault that lost too many men along the way would falter, sometimes just yards short of the goal.

Infantrymen took the overwhelming majority of the deaths and casualties in the war. In the deciding moments of a battle, they sometimes stood only yards apart, pouring fire into one another at point-blank range until one side broke the other's will to fight.

Rolled Blanket: Confederate infantrymen tended to carry less equipment than Union troops, partly because the Confederacy had a harder time keeping its soldiers supplied. Most favored a rolled blanket over a knapsack.

Battle of Gettysburg: A Currier & Ives lithograph of the infantry battle on July 3, 1863.

Day 2–July 2–Midnight

Meade's Headquarters

July 2 was a day of hard fighting. The two armies suffered some 19,000 casualties. But while the Union army had suffered heavy losses, by the end of the day, it still held all the key terrain. Its position remained intact.

That night, Union General George Meade held a council of war at Lydia Leister's house, located behind Union lines. Meade was cautious, but his confidence was growing. The Confederates had again nearly won the day, but the Union army had turned back one of the largest attacks of the war. When Meade learned that his army had captured soldiers from every division except General George Pickett's, he knew he had faced nearly the entire Army of Northern Virginia.

The Union commanders discussed options for the next day, from moving the army to counterattacking Lee. By midnight they had agreed unanimously to stay put on the high ground, remain on the defensive, and fight it out.

Meade's Headquarters: General Meade set up headquarters at this simple farmhouse along Cemetery Ridge, where widow Lydia Leister lived with her five children.

Day 3–July 3–Morning

The Best Laid Plans

In the early morning of the third day, the Confederates held a tenuous foothold at the base of Culp's Hill and faced the Union lines across the rest of the battlefield. Before catching a few hours sleep, Confederate General

Union Rear: This Edwin Forbes painting of the Union rear depicts the Battle of Gettysburg on its third day. Cemetery Hill is visible in the left background, while Culp's Hill can be seen on the far right.

Robert E. Lee ordered generals Ewell and Longstreet to renew their attacks at dawn. Lee's army had come so close to victory—one more determined attack might end it. But Longstreet was opposed to attacking again on his front. Meanwhile, the Union army struck first, attacking at Culp's Hill, undoing Lee's plans. The two sides fought along the slopes of Culp's Hill for nearly seven hours.

Cartridges: A box of cartridges for Sharps rifles, a popular weapon among U.S. sharpshooters.

DAY 3–JULY 3–1:00 P.M.

LONGSTREET'S CRISIS

With his original plan gone awry, General Lee determined to launch a major attack on the Union center on Cemetery Ridge, using General George Pickett's fresh division and other troops from General A. P. Hill's corps. Lee selected Longstreet to command the attack, but Longstreet believed it was doomed. "General," he said to Lee, "it is my opinion that no 15,000 men ever arrayed for battle can take that position." Lee's plan called for a massive artillery barrage followed by an infantry attack by nearly 13,500 men. It was a great gamble for victory.

DAY 3–JULY 3–3:30 P.M.

PICKETT'S CHARGE

Confederate General George Pickett and Gettysburg are linked forever. But Pickett's Charge could go by a number of names. Robert E. Lee ordered it. James Longstreet directed it. Johnston Pettigrew and Isaac Trimble each led a Confederate division. And Union General Winfield Hancock commanded most of the forces that turned back the assault.

Pickett's Charge was preceded by the largest artillery bombardment in the Western Hemisphere. Some 160 Confederate cannon opened up on the center of Cemetery Ridge, and nearly 100 Union guns answered. After two hours, thousands of Confederates advanced from their positions along Seminary Ridge.

General George E. Pickett: As they charged the Union army, Pickett famously told his men, "Up, men, and to your posts! Don't forget today that you are from old Virginia!"

As the Army of Northern Virginia began to walk toward the Union lines on Cemetery Ridge in the nearly 90-degree heat, their line was almost a mile wide. No Union soldier ever forgot the sight. The Confederates aimed for an area a few hundred yards wide near a copse of trees along Cemetery Ridge. The attackers slowed to climb the stout fences along Emmitsburg Road, coming within range of Union infantrymen on Cemetery Ridge. Minié balls began to take a toll on the attackers. In about 30 minutes, the Confederates covered the ground between the two armies, briefly broke through the Union lines, and then fell back. Nearly half of them were killed, wounded, or captured in the attack.

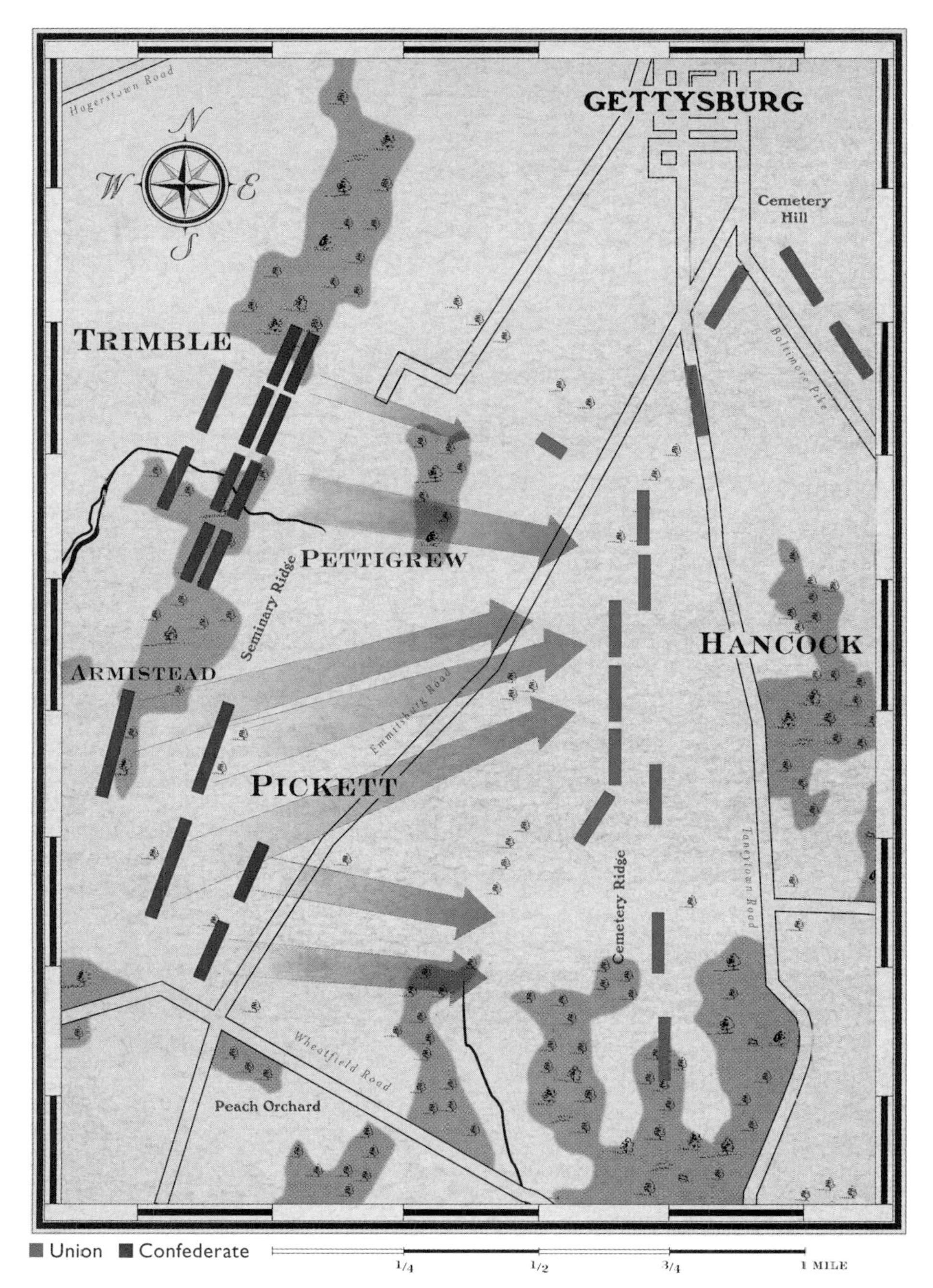

■ Union ■ Confederate

1/4 1/2 3/4 1 MILE

Day Three: On the afternoon of July 3, 1863, Confederate General George Pickett attacked Union General Winfield Hancock's lines on Cemetery Ridge. The Confederates, who marched across an open field to launch the attack, were held firm by Union troops.

DAY 3–JULY 3–AFTERNOON

The Cavalry Fight

As Pickett's men marched toward the stone wall on Cemetery Ridge, nearly 7,000 cavalrymen clashed three miles east of Gettysburg. Confederate General J. E. B. Stuart had led his division to a position where he hoped to strike the rear of the Union army, but he found 3,500 Union cavalry under General David Gregg barring his way.

The two sides engaged in sharp skirmishing in the mid-afternoon until finally Stuart attempted to break through with a mounted attack. The clash of the mounted men, wrote Union Captain William Miller, "[was] a crash like the falling of timber." Stuart was checked, and that evening he withdrew his command.

Cavalry Battle: On July 3, thousands of cavalrymen battled a few miles outside Gettysburg. The Civil War changed the cavalry. The traditional ideal of the dashing horseman, sword in hand, didn't survive even the first months of the war. Massed infantry with modern rifles were more than a match for a cavalry charge.

Sharps Carbine: Long, muzzle-loading rifles were the standard weapon of infantrymen, but they were too cumbersome to carry on horseback. Cavalrymen carried lighter and shorter weapons called carbines, such as this Sharps version from the 1860s.

Day 3–July 3–Late Afternoon

Is the Battle Over?

The survivors of Pickett's Charge retreated to the shelter of the trees on Seminary Ridge. As the Confederates fell back, cheering began up and down the Union lines. Union General George Meade was encouraged but still wary. Meanwhile, Robert E. Lee awaited a Union counterattack. Both sides dug in, prepared to fight again. No one in Gettysburg, soldier or civilian, knew what would come next.

Leaving Gettysburg: Thousands of Confederate soldiers retreated from Gettysburg the night of July 3.

At dusk, the armies returned to the positions they had held for most of the day, waiting. An uneasy calm settled over Gettysburg that evening. Most people kept off the streets. Around midnight, said a young Henry Jacobs, "the streets began to fill with men." Other residents heard the sound of wagons. Under the cover of darkness, the Army of Northern Virginia was leaving Gettysburg.

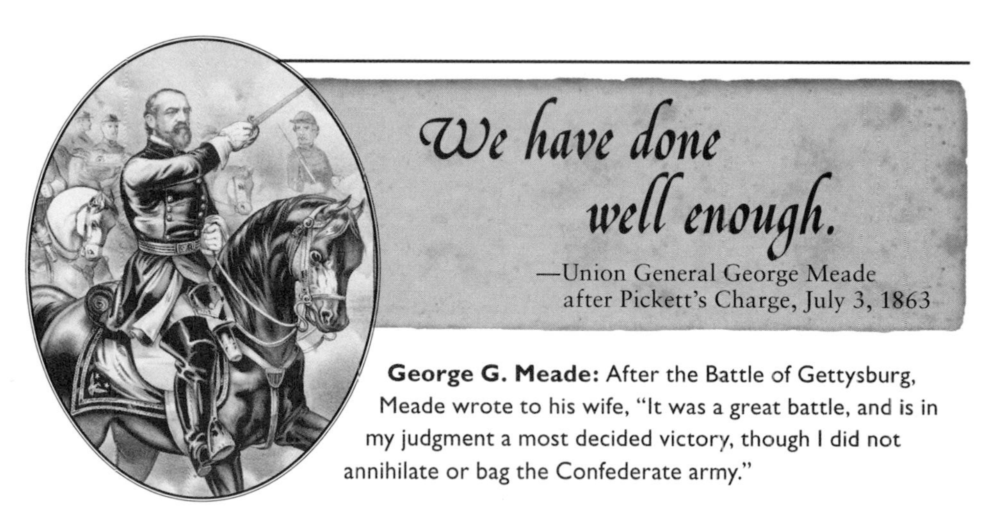

George G. Meade: After the Battle of Gettysburg, Meade wrote to his wife, "It was a great battle, and is in my judgment a most decided victory, though I did not annihilate or bag the Confederate army."

Civil War Guns and Artillery

The primary weapon of the early Civil War was either a smoothbore musket (meaning that the ball of the bullet was discharged from a smooth, hollow barrel) or a rifled musket (meaning that the bullet spun in the barrel when fired). Smoothbore muskets had a much shorter range and were far less accurate than rifled muskets, which could fire three rounds per minute and hit targets more than a half mile away. By July 1863, the smoothbore musket had been mostly phased out. At Gettysburg, only 15 percent of the Union army carried smoothbore muskets. Most infantrymen carried muzzle-loading rifled muskets, such as the more modern Springfield or Enfield varieties. At about nine pounds, Civil War rifles and muskets were heavy, and took 20 to 30 seconds to reload. The majority of combat injuries were caused by these weapons.

Revolver: Many soldiers brought their own handguns into battle, such as this .36 caliber "Adams Navy" revolver made by the Massachusetts Army Co.

Culp's Hill: This monument to the 111th Pennsylvania Infantry Regiment stands on Culp's Hill, where a storm of gunfire ripped through the trees the night of July 2.

While infantrymen carried rifles and muskets, cavalrymen favored carbines—short-barreled rifles that were lighter and easier to handle on horseback. They also carried sabers and revolvers. Some riders carried four or five revolvers tucked in their belts, clothing, or saddle. At Gettysburg, the Union's cavalry corps alone carried more than 10,000 handguns.

Handguns were standard issue to cavalrymen, but officers had to purchase their own. Civil War officers used single-shot pistols or five- and six-shot revolvers as their primary weapons of defense. Artillerymen carried them as secondary weapons. Unlike muskets and rifles, revolvers were effective mainly at very close range. A well-handled revolver would disable an enemy before he got close enough to use his sword.

Soldiers of Invention: From the early days of the Civil War, soldiers took the equipment they were given, used it, modified it, and sometimes threw it away. Rifles became tent poles and flattened bullets passed as poker chips.

Firearms of all types were in short supply at the beginning of the war. As both sides strained to meet the demands for arms, many early volunteers were issued antiquated, imported, and nearly obsolete weapons. Eventually, though, a few quality types were obtained in large numbers and became standard issue to the soldiers of both armies.

War Weapons

The firearms displayed here represent some of the variety of weapons—both domestic and import—used by both armies at the Battle of Gettysburg.

Carbine
Richmond, Confederate Manufacture, .58 caliber

Breechloading Carbine
Smith, .50 caliber

Breechloading Carbine
Sharps, New Model 1859, .52 caliber

Breechloading Carbine
Merill, 2nd Type, .54 caliber

Breechloading Carbine
Gallagher, .50 caliber

Revolver
Smith and Wesson,
Model No. 2 Army, .32 caliber

Revolver
Samuel Colt,
Model 1860 Army, .44 caliber

Revolver
Kerr, Double Action,
Type 2, .44 caliber

Breechloading Carbine
Burnside, 2nd Model, .54 caliber

Breechloading Carbine
Hall-North, Model 1840, Type 2, .52 caliber

Breechloading Carbine
Warner, .50 caliber

Breechloading Carbine
Maynard, Model 1863, .50 caliber

Revolver and Stock
Samuel Colt, Model 1848 Army,
.44 caliber

Pepperbox Pistol
Sharps, Model 1B,
.22 caliber

Pistol
New Haven Arms,
Volvanic Lever Action, .31 caliber

Revolver
Savage, Navy Model,
.44 caliber

Revolver
Perrin, Model 1860,
French Manufacture, .45 caliber

Pepperbox Revolver
English Manufacture, c. 1840
.31 caliber

Equipping the Artillery

Artillery could be found in every arena of the Civil War, from heavy artillery mounted on ships and in fortifications to light artillery that accompanied armies in the field. Union and Confederate forces used more than forty different models of field pieces. But while the size, shape, weight, range, and projectiles of the artillery varied greatly during the war, only light artillery, both rifled and smoothbore, was used at Gettysburg.

Cemetery Ridge: A monument to Battery A, 4th United States Artillery, stands at the site of Pickett's Charge. As the Confederate attackers reached Cemetery Ridge, they tried to capture the cannon defending the area.

Shell: This three-inch shell from an Ordnance Rifle was found on the battlefield of Gettysburg.

Civil War batteries required a great deal of specialized equipment to keep their guns cool and clear of debris and to ensure they functioned properly. They also required specialized equipment for aiming, loading, and firing cannon.

There is no nonsense about us . . .
We have been in the service long enough
to know that fighting is no child's play.

—Private E. D. Benedict, 12th Pennsylvania Reserves, July 1, 1863

Union Battery: Maintaining the cannon in a battery was an important job, and discipline in the artillery was very strict due to the value of the weapon.

Projectiles were manufactured using sand-filled molds and produced one at a time. There were four basic types of projectiles: solid shot, shell, case shot (or shrapnel), and canister. Each had a specific purpose on the battlefield. Spherical projectiles were used in smoothbore cannon, such as the popular Napoleon cannon, while the conical projectiles were for rifled guns. The most accurate fire, however, came from long-range rifled cannon. Due to its strong manufacturing ability, the North had a greater number of rifled cannon and guns, and thus had an advantage with its artillery.

Grease Bucket: Artillerymen carried this bucket at Gettysburg to grease the wheels and axles of their cannon.

Deadly Equipment

These pages contain examples of Civil War projectiles and the equipment troops needed to sustain their artillery.

Case Shot
Hotchkiss Pattern
14 lb James Rifle

Solid Shot
12 lb Napoleon
Smoothbore Gun

Case Shot
10 lb Parrott Gun

Case Shot
Burton Pattern
3" Ordnance Rifle
Confederate Manufacture

Case Shot
12 lb Napoleon
Smoothbore Gun
Confederate Manufacture

Case Shot
12 lb Napoleon
Smoothbore Gun
Confederate Manufacture

Canister Round
Hotchkiss Pattern
3" Ordnance Rifle

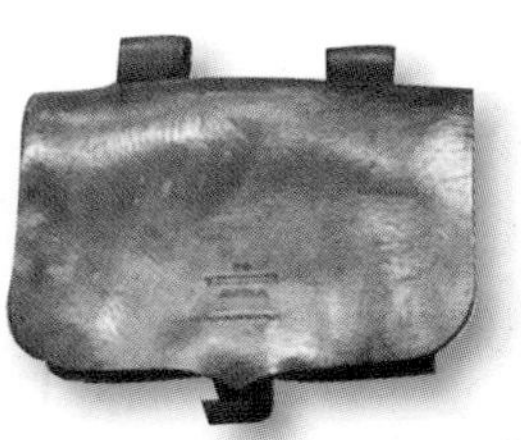

Gunner's Pouch
To carry fuses

Shell
12 lb Smoothbore Gun
Confederate Manufacture

Fuse Gimlet
To remove debris from vent in breech

Wire Gunner's Pick
To puncture powder bag

Shell
Read Pattern
10 lb Parrott Gun
Confederate Manufacture

Case Shot
20 lb Parrott Gun

Solid Shot
Britten Pattern
12 lb Blakley Rifle
English Manufacture

Sponge and Rammer
To cool and load the cannon

Worm
To clean tube

Solid Shot
10 lb 3" Ordnance Rifle
or 10 lb Parrott Gun

Solid Shot
12 lb Whitworth Rifle
English Manufacture

Shell
20 lb Parrott Rifle
Confederate Manufacture

Shell
Hotchkiss Pattern
3.67" Ordnance Rifle

Shell
Archer Pattern
3" Ordnance Rifle
Confederate Manufacture

Case Shot
14 lb James Rifle

Solid Shot
Read Pattern
3" Ordnance Rifle
Confederate Manufacture

Shell
Britten
12 lb Blakley Rifle
English Manufacture

Case Shot
Read Pattern
3" Ordnance Rifle
Confederate Manufacture

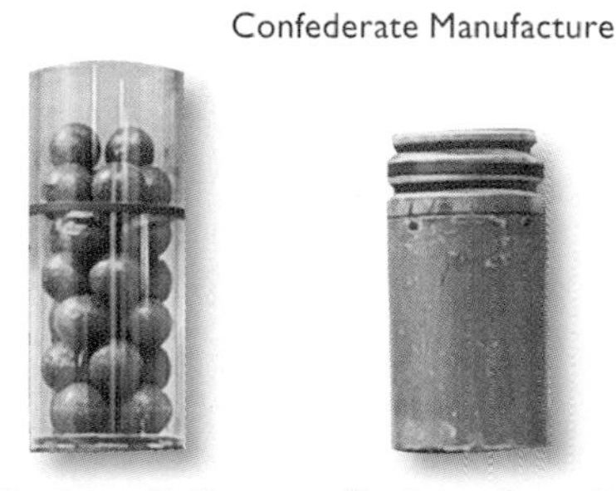

Canister Balls

Canister Round
6 lb Smoothbore Gun

The Army of Northern Virginia started its retreat on July 4 in a driving rain, while the Army of the Potomac began a cautious pursuit the next day. During the retreat from Gettysburg, more than 2,000 Confederate soldiers were taken prisoner by Union forces.

The Union army caught up to the Confederates near the Potomac River. Lee's army was dug in, but Meade decided to risk an attack. At the last minute, however, Meade decided the Confederate position was too strong and canceled it. The Union troops advanced on the morning of July 14 but found only empty entrenchments. Lee's army had withdrawn to Virginia.

Signal Lantern: Objects such as lanterns—used by signalmen to broadcast their messages—were strewn across Gettysburg after the battle.

Confederate Retreat: General Robert E. Lee's bold strike into Pennsylvania ended as his army filed across the Potomac River into Virginia 10 days after the Battle of Gettysburg.

Beyond Gettysburg

The Battle of Gettysburg changed both armies and the course of the war as well as the small town in southern Pennsylvania. The battle dashed the Confederates' expectations of another victory and sent the Army of Northern Virginia in full retreat. It also brought the Union its greatest triumph of the war and a renewed faith that the nation might prevail in the end. The possibility of peace negotiations all but disappeared.

Siege of Vicksburg: In May and June 1863, General Ulysses S. Grant's armies converged on Vicksburg, a vital Confederate stronghold on the Mississippi River. After a prolonged siege, Vicksburg surrendered on July 4, 1863, and the Confederacy was effectively split in half.

On July 4, the river town of Vicksburg, Mississippi, surrendered to the army of Union General Ulysses S. Grant. For the first time since the war began, the Union controlled the Mississippi River. The North, however, was beginning to show the strain of the war. One week later, thousands of New Yorkers rioted in the streets, angry at the endless casualty lists, a draft that favored the rich, and a war for emancipation. They feared that freed slaves might come north and compete for their jobs, and they lynched several black residents of the city.

The North had gained some stunning victories, but those triumphs had come at a price. Meanwhile, the South remained strong. The war was far from over.

CASUALTIES

In many Civil War battles, both sides had almost an equal number of casualties. Winning a battle often cost nearly as many lives as losing one. To be counted among the wounded, a soldier had to be injured severely enough to require the care of a doctor. Thousands of lightly injured men weren't officially considered casualties.

> *Thousands of our brave boys are left upon the enemy's soil and in my opinion our army will never be made of such material again.*
>
> —Private Alexander McNeill, 2nd South Carolina Infantry, July 7, 1863

The Battle of Gettysburg ended with 23,000 Union casualties. Of these, 3,155 soldiers were killed, 14,529 were wounded, and 5,365 were captured or missing. The Confederate army did not compile accurate or complete casualty figures of its losses, and the confusion after the battle made estimates difficult. The most reliable numbers put the Confederacy's losses at 28,000 casualties—approximately 3,500 soldiers killed, 18,000 wounded, and 6,500 captured or missing.

The Slaughter Pen: Scores of dead Confederate soldiers lay at the base of Little Round Top after the fighting on July 2. "The dead literally covered the ground," remembered Confederate Colonel William C. Oates. "The blood stood in puddles on the rocks."

Reclaiming the Town

All afternoon on July 4, 1863, it rained on the living and the dead in Gettysburg. People saw a landscape ravaged by cannon shells, wagon wheels, and the rush of armies. Hundreds of dead horses lay among the dead men, and the cries of the wounded rose up amid the stench of death.

For the townspeople, army medical staff, and volunteers, a second battle had just begun. Roughly 21,000 men from the two armies lay wounded in temporary field hospitals at Gettysburg. The Confederate army left behind about 7,000 men too severely injured to move. Another 6,000 to 7,000 Confederate wounded were carried west in a wagon train that stretched about 17 miles long. Hundreds of these soldiers never made it back to Virginia. Many were captured along the way, while others fell behind, got lost, or climbed out of the wagons to die by the wayside.

Broken China: This pitcher was found at the Forney farm, the site of vicious fighting on the first day. After the battle, John Forney filed a claim for damages to his property with the U.S. government. There is no record of whether he was paid.

Burials: Bodies of dead Confederate soldiers gathered for burial near the woods bordering the Wheatfield. In just a few hours on July 2, nearly 4,000 soldiers became casualties in this action.

Soon after the battle, the Army of the Potomac and most of its medical corps left Gettysburg to pursue the retreating Confederates. The responsibility of caring for the wounded fell to a small number of army surgeons, aide organizations such as the Sanitary Commission and Christian Commission, and the people of Gettysburg and Adams County. It would be four months before the last of the wounded were removed from Gettysburg's field hospitals.

Hallowed Ground

Almost all the buildings in Gettysburg were still standing after the three-day battle. The town and the lives of its people, however, were changed forever. Residents lost their possessions, and some, their livelihoods. Heavy army wagons and artillery vehicles tore up roads. Soldiers ransacked homes for food, clothing, and valuables. Outside town, several barns and farmhouses burned to the ground.

Union Canteen: A soldier from the 83rd Pennsylvania Infantry left this canteen on the slopes of Little Round Top.

Battle Wreckage: Broken battery caissons and dead horses covered the ground of Cemetery Ridge, the site of Pickett's Charge.

Most significantly, the townspeople faced the horror of thousands of dead and wounded. They found blood in their homes where the wounded had lain. And they saw their town and the farms around it changed into something new—hallowed ground dotted with broken fences, tumbled stone walls, and dead horses. The battlefield became a grisly combination of graveyard, hospital ward, and tourist attraction. Thousands of civilians looked for loved ones, gawked at corpses, or combed the fields for souvenirs. The job of guarding the battlefield and the Confederate prisoners fell to a few hundred Union soldiers.

Tons of wreckage, scrap metal, curiosities, and souvenirs—including 30,000 to 40,000 weapons—were left behind. The Union army collected most of the rifles and other equipment from the battlefield, but some residents snuck off with souvenirs, directly violating the orders of the Union army.

A Hospital Town

As soon as the battle had begun, the wounded from both sides started to fill Gettysburg's homes, offices, stores, barns, and other buildings. By July 3, more than 100 buildings in and around Gettysburg held wounded soldiers. "The whole town is one vast hospital," wrote one nurse, "all public and a great many private buildings full of sufferers."

> *The citizens of Gettysburg behaved nobly . . . They came out of their cellars and immediately applied themselves to the relief of the wounded.*
>
> —John B. Linn, visitor to Gettysburg, July 1863

Thousands of people streamed into town for months after the battle. To help keep the peace, the Union provost marshal prohibited the sale of beer and liquor in Gettysburg after 9:00 p.m. The battle and its aftermath brought out the best in most people. A few found ways to exploit the situation, such as selling bread or water or charging a wounded soldier for a wagon ride to a hospital, but most local residents were immensely generous, serving as cooks, nurses, hosts, and guides for families looking for loved ones.

2nd Corps Hospital: This rare photograph of the 2nd Corps field hospital was taken in July 1863. After the battle, the tents at this hospital held 2,500 wounded soldiers.

MEDICINE OF THE BATTLEFIELD

Gettysburg's 51,000 casualties—indicating those killed, wounded, captured, or missing—made it the bloodiest battle of the war. At Gettysburg, about 4,000 of those wounded died of injury or secondary infection. Most men fell to the rifles and muskets of their enemies, rather than by artillery shells or cannon. By design, the soft lead bullets flattened as they hit, shattering bones and shredding flesh and muscle.

Confederate Surgeon: Southern surgeons, such as the one pictured here, were often undersupplied.

In the days after the battle, surgeons at Gettysburg operated around the clock, often by the light of lanterns in the open air. Union surgeons set up one field hospital at the Weikert farm, just east of the Round Tops, where they operated at the kitchen table. Civil War surgeons usually worked in bloodstained clothes, using the same saws and knives on patient after patient. To locate bullets, they used probes—and often their fingers. Antibiotics were unknown, and infections ran rampant in the hot, damp open-air wards. They had some useful medicines, however, such as chloroform, ether, opium, and alcohol to ease pain. Few soldiers on either side endured an amputation without an anesthetic.

The surgeons grew skillful by grim repetition. They knew almost nothing about viruses, bacteria, infections, and the spread of most diseases. They often worked in miserable conditions and sometimes under fire. But they saved the lives of thousands of soldiers with quick treatment, simple instruments, and skillful technique.

Surgical Saw: Civil War surgeons amputated tens of thousands of limbs with saws like this and saved as many lives.

Landscape of the Wounded

Dozens of field hospitals were spread across Gettysburg in tents, barns, churches, homes, and under the shade of trees. Confederate hospitals were spread north and west of town, Union hospitals were located south and east. In mid-July, a new general hospital, Camp Letterman, was set up east of town, and one by one the field hospitals closed. The new hospital was named for Jonathan Letterman, commander of the Army of the Potomac's medical department. Surgeons, stewards, nurses, and volunteers tended to more than 4,000 Union and Confederate patients at the hospital over the next four months. The hospital saved the lives of many Union and Confederate soldiers.

Camp Letterman: This general hospital was established east of Gettysburg in mid July. Several thousand wounded were treated here until the hospital closed in November 1863.

The Spangler Farm

Located behind the Union line on Cemetery Hill and bound by two local roads, the George Spangler Farm served as the 11th Corps' field hospital during the Battle of Gettysburg. After the battle, the farm continued to serve as a hospital for wounded soldiers on both sides—including Lewis Armistead, one of the Confederacy's most important generals, who died at the farm from his wounds. The adjoining barn housed Union and Confederate soldiers who had undergone surgery. The Spangler Farm treated more than 1,400 wounded soldiers on both sides until mid-August 1863.

Medicine Bottle: During the Civil War, the U.S. Sanitary Commission and the U.S. Christian Commission saved many lives, bringing medicine, bandages, food, and comfort to soldiers.

Spangler Farm: The Spangler Farm served as a field hospital for both Union and Confederate troops. In 2008, the Gettysburg Foundation purchased the 80-acre farm as part of its partnership with the National Park Service. The land is now preserved and not threatened by development.

Prisoners, Deserters, and Stragglers

As the Army of Northern Virginia left Gettysburg, hundreds of deserters or stragglers snuck off or fell behind. Plenty of Union soldiers did the same. After the battle, the two armies held some 12,000 prisoners of war. About 4,000 Union soldiers began the long trek south with the Army of Northern Virginia. Confederate prisoners were marched to a railroad at Westminster, Maryland, then moved to their final destination prison camps anywhere from Maryland to Illinois.

> *Today is Independence Day. I do not feel very independent, though. I should think I was rather dependant, as I am a prisoner of war and I am dependant on somebody to get me out of this scrape.*
>
> —Private William H. Warren, 17th Connecticut Infantry, July 4, 1863

Approximately 400,000 soldiers and sailors would pass through roughly 150 prison camps by the end of the Civil War. Some 50,000 men—about 13 percent—died there. At first, the two armies set up a parole system for exchanging prisoners. Prisoners were released if they promised not to fight again until they were exchanged for enemy prisoners. The Union also allowed Confederate prisoners to regain their freedom by taking an oath of allegiance to the United States. General Robert E. Lee offered paroles to captured U.S. soldiers at Gettysburg. More than a thousand Union men took him up on it, while thousands more refused. By then the system had nearly broken down. The cost of the war grew deeper every day, and any cooperation between the two sides was difficult.

Confederate Prisoners: Thousands of Confederate soldiers were captured as Lee's army retreated from Gettysburg. Many waited out the war at a prison camp in Point Lookout, Maryland.

The Dead

Roughly 7,000 men died on the battlefield at Gettysburg in three days of fighting—almost three times the population of the town. Their bodies were spread over 25 square miles. No one there, soldier or civilian, had seen death on this scale. Gettysburg was the deadliest battle of the war.

Most men were buried near where they fell, often by soldiers of their own regiment. Comrades wrote the names and units of the soldiers they knew, or could identify from some clue on the body, on temporary headboards and laid the boards over the bodies. By July 6, most of the dead lay in temporary graves.

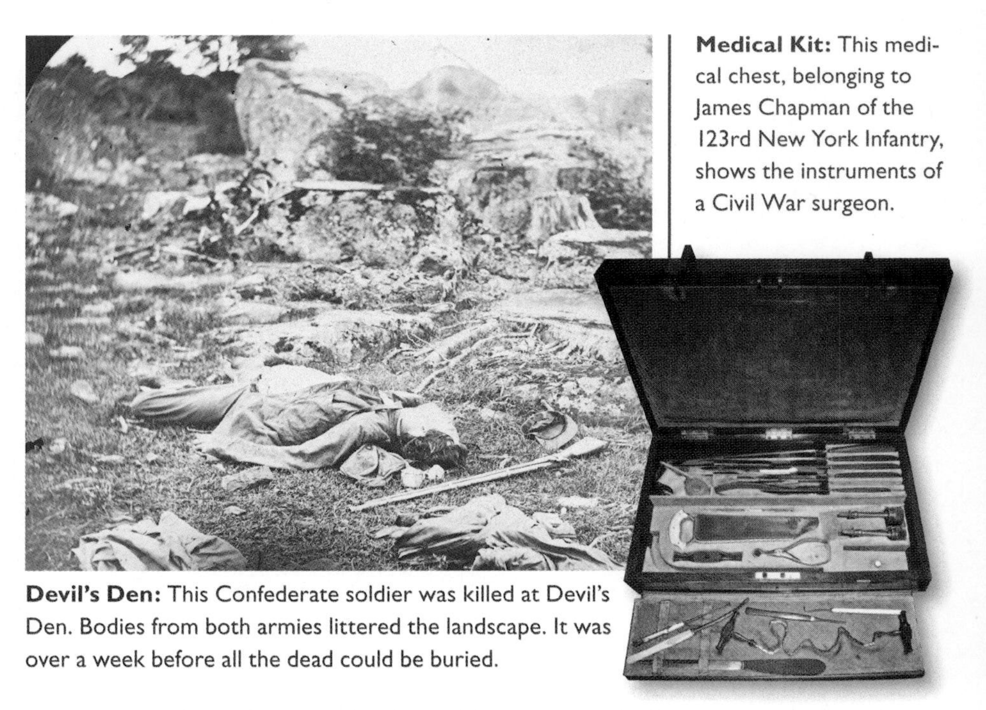

Medical Kit: This medical chest, belonging to James Chapman of the 123rd New York Infantry, shows the instruments of a Civil War surgeon.

Devil's Den: This Confederate soldier was killed at Devil's Den. Bodies from both armies littered the landscape. It was over a week before all the dead could be buried.

Thousands of Confederate dead would remain in shallow graves for nearly a decade before their remains were shipped South. The Union army spent little time identifying Confederate corpses, but one doctor, J. W. C. O'Neal of Gettysburg, kept invaluable records of the number and location of Confederate dead. His notes helped scores of Southern families find their loved ones.

The gravesites were temporary for several reasons: The farmers of Adams County needed to reclaim their fields, orchards, and pastures, and some leading citizens of the town wanted a fitting burial site for the fallen Union soldiers. After October 1863, 3,556 of the approximately 5,200 Union dead were buried in the Soldiers' National Cemetery. The rest were claimed by their families and taken to their hometowns.

The Soldiers' National Cemetery

The new Soldiers' National Cemetery in Gettysburg was a resting place for the Union dead and a first step toward helping the North heal from the battle. For the main address at the dedication ceremonies, prominent Gettysburg citizen David Wills chose a well-known statesman—Edward Everett of Massachusetts. Wills also sent an invitation to Abraham Lincoln to add "a few appropriate remarks."

Dedication March: Abraham Lincoln rode in this procession to the dedication ceremony of the Soldiers' National Cemetery.

Lincoln drew on the Declaration of Independence to draft the Gettysburg Address. Despite decades of conflict and the secession of the Southern states, he declared, Americans were one people. The Civil War was a test of this belief. It was also a test of whether a nation dedicated to the proposition that all men are created equal could survive. In Lincoln's eyes, a loss by the United States would mean the end of the American experiment in democratic self-government.

In a few words, Lincoln redefined for the North, and eventually for all Americans, the meaning and value of the struggle for a unified nation. The Gettysburg Address became what many consider to be the best summation of the values that America believes in and stands for.

I should be glad . . . that I came as near to the central idea of the occasion in two hours as you did in two minutes.

—Edward Everett to Abraham Lincoln, November 20, 1863

Four score and seven years ago our fathers brought forth on this continent, a new nation, conceived in Liberty, and dedicated to the proposition that all men are created equal.

Now we are engaged in a great civil war, testing whether that nation, or any nation so conceived and so dedicated, can long endure. We are met on a great battle-field of that war. We have come to dedicate a portion of that field, as a final resting place for those who here gave their lives that that nation might live. It is altogether fitting and proper that we should do this.

But, in a larger sense, we can not dedicate—we can not consecrate—we can not hallow—this ground. The brave men, living and dead, who struggled here, have consecrated it, far above our poor power to add or detract. The world will little note, nor long remember what we say here, but it can never forget what they did here.

It is for us the living, rather, to be dedicated here to the unfinished work which they who fought here have thus far so nobly advanced. It is rather for us to be here dedicated to the great task remaining before us—that from these honored dead we take increased devotion to that cause for which they gave the last full measure of devotion—that we here highly resolve that these dead shall not have died in vain—that this nation, under God, shall have a new birth of freedom—and that government of the people, by the people, for the people, shall not perish from the earth.

Dedication Ceremonies: In this rare photograph of the dedication ceremonies at the Soldiers' National Cemetery, a blurred image of Abraham Lincoln is visible to the left of the man in the top hat and sash. Some 15,000 people attended the event.

Presidential Portrait: Abraham Lincoln is pictured here less than a week before giving the Gettysburg Address. The speech was applauded by papers that supported his administration and vigorously attacked by those opposed.

After the Battle of Gettysburg, the Civil War was still little more than halfway through its course; nearly half the war's casualties lay ahead. The nation's great suffering pulled the American people in different directions. Millions were ready for the bloodshed to end—in one nation or two, with slavery or without. Others were even more determined to win the war. Anything short of victory would betray the horrible sacrifices so far. So the war dragged on. No one knew when it might end.

FRANK LESLIE'S
ILLUSTRATED
NEWSPAPER

NEW YORK, MAY 21, 1864.

The War—The Beginning of the End.

Media Coverage: The April 8, 1864, front page of *Frank Leslie's Illustrated Newspaper* covered the fighting in Mansfield, Louisiana.

By 1864, Southerners faced extreme exhaustion and economic ruin. Thousands of refugees took to Southern roads, many headed toward cities that were already overcrowded. Both civilians and soldiers went hungry. Northern industry, however, boomed. Newspaper stories and veterans, rather than the sound of gunfire, brought the war home. Thousands of Northerners worked to supply the Union army with food, uniforms, rifles, and ammunition, and to lay hundreds of miles of new railroad track.

The War of Attrition

The Confederacy's best hope was to persuade the people of the United States that there was no end in sight. For months, the Confederate army succeeded in trading lost ground for staggering Union casualties—nearly 40,000 in May 1864. In an assault at Cold Harbor, Virginia, roughly 7,000 Union soldiers were killed or wounded in a single day. The military's need for manpower seemed inexhaustible, and the toll demoralized Northerners. A hundred thousand soldiers left the Union army when their enlistments expired in 1864. They were replaced by men drafted into the army or ordered to volunteer with bounties. Meanwhile, desertions steadily thinned Confederate ranks.

Draft Notice: This Pennsylvania draft notice, dated May 24, 1864, called for another 700,000 Union soldiers.

Election of 1864

The Union elections of November 1864 were among the most important in the nation's history. In them, white Southerners placed their dwindling hopes for independence. They knew that support was eroding for Lincoln and the Republicans, and the Democrats were calling for an immediate cease-fire and peace negotiations. If Lincoln lost, the South might have the possibility of a negotiated peace and an independent Confederacy.

Then in September, the army of Union General William Tecumseh Sherman captured Atlanta, Georgia, and General Philip Sheridan drove the Confederate army from Virginia's Shenandoah Valley. Northerners thought they saw the beginning of the end, and Lincoln's prospects changed almost overnight.

Nineteen states allowed soldiers to cast their ballots in the field. They voted overwhelmingly for Lincoln. Lincoln won in an electoral landslide, 212 to 21. The popular vote was closer, 2.2 million to 1.8 million, or about 55 to 45 percent. No U.S. president had won a second term since Andrew Jackson 30 years before.

Campaign Poster: A campaign poster for 1864 Republican presidential candidate Abraham Lincoln and running mate Andrew Johnson. Until the tide of the war changed in September 1864, Lincoln was not optimistic about his chances for reelection.

> *I cannot afford to give three years of my life to maintaining this nation and then give the Rebels all they want.*
>
> —Union soldier on the election of 1864

Appomattox

On April 2, 1865, after a siege of nine months, the Army of the Potomac began to break through the Confederate defenses that ringed Richmond and Petersburg. The Army of Northern Virginia gave way, and a weeklong chase began. The Union army pursued the Confederates west to the little town of Appomattox Court House. The Confederate army melted away until Robert E. Lee finally surrendered on April 9.

Lee's Surrender: On April 9, 1865, General Robert E. Lee surrendered to Union General Ulysses S. Grant in the parlor of Wilmer and Virginia McClean's home in rural Appomattox Court House, Virginia. There, Grant promised to allow Lee's Confederate soldiers to keep their horses and mules and arranged for 25,000 rations to be sent to the hungry Southern troops. The two met there again the following day to finalize terms.

With General Order No. 9, Lee informed the soldiers of his army that their war was over. The news spread quickly by telegraph, and celebrations erupted across the North the next day. Union General Ulysses S. Grant gave 25,000 rations to the starving Confederates and agreed to let Lee's men keep their horses. "The war is over," said Grant. "The rebels are our countrymen again."

Brick: This brick comes from the McClean home in Appomattox Court House, where Robert E. Lee and Ulysses S. Grant drew up a peace agreement, ending four bloody years of conflict. The home was designated a National Historical Monument in 1940.

Lincoln's Assassination

Abraham Lincoln had only five days to rest from his labors in reuniting the nation. On the evening of April 11, 1865—just two days after General Robert E. Lee surrendered at Appomattox—Lincoln gave his last speech from the balcony of the White House. He spoke to the crowd below about readmitting the states of the Confederacy to the Union, saying, "Let us all join in doing the acts necessary to restoring the proper practical relations between these states and the Union." Three days later, on April 14, John Wilkes Booth assassinated him at Ford's Theatre in Washington, D.C.

Abraham Lincoln's Gettysburg Address honored the men who gave "the last full measure of devotion" to save the Union. In the end, it was his own eulogy.

The Assassination: This illustration of Lincoln's assassination shows (from right to left) Booth, Lincoln, Mary Lincoln, and their guests Clara Harris and Major Henry Rathbone.

The Cost of War

After the war, soldiers on both sides returned home, some as heroes, some as invalids—nearly all as changed men. Union soldiers came home to celebrations of a great victory, though at a great price. Confederate soldiers bore the burdens of defeat, widespread poverty, and the end of a way of life across the South. The South would take nearly a century to recover from the devastation of the war. Nearly one-quarter of all Southern white men—approximately 258,000—were dead.

Results of War

The Civil War ended a deep-seated national conflict forever. The United States was one nation, indivisible—not a collection of states, each free to secede. Now Americans had to find a way to move beyond their bitterness and rebuild the nation they shared.

The end of the war brought sweeping changes. The national government grew immensely in influence, and the United States became an international power. Farms, businesses, and industries in the North thrived, while much of the South lay in ruins. Four million people enslaved at the beginning of the Civil War were freed at its end, changing forever an old way of life in the United States. The end of the war brought the passage of the 13th Amendment, which abolished slavery, and the 14th Amendment, which granted citizenship to African Americans. For the first time in more than 200 years, America was the land of the free.

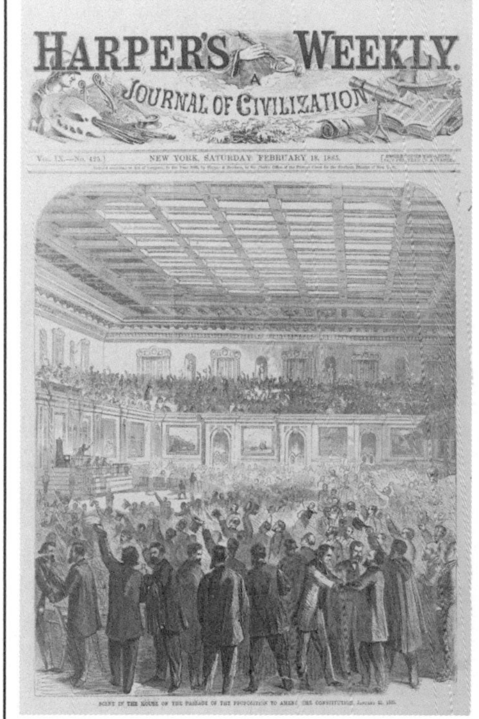
HARPER'S WEEKLY.
A JOURNAL OF CIVILIZATION
NEW YORK, SATURDAY, FEBRUARY 18, 1865.

Passing the Proposition: The January 31, 1865, issue of *Harper's Weekly* covered the House's passage of the 13th Amendment.

With malice toward none, with charity for all, with firmness in the right as God gives us to see the right, let us strive on to finish the work we are in, to bind up the nation's wounds.

—Abraham Lincoln, Second Inaugural Address, March 4, 1865

Battlefield People and Places

The Soldiers' National Monument: Union General George Meade spoke at the dedication of the Soldiers' National Monument on July 1, 1869. The figure of Lady Liberty stands atop the monument, while tributes to "War," "History," "Plenty," and "Peace" surround the base.

The first monument at Gettysburg was erected at the Soldiers' National Cemetery in 1869. The simple memorial urn honors the 1st Minnesota Infantry, which suffered extreme losses during its desperate charge on July 2, 1863. As the years went on, veterans placed more monuments and markers in locations where their units had fought. The memorials were generally erected in the center of that unit's formation, with flank markers—small, square stones—indicating the ends of the line. At first, many Union veterans objected to having Confederate monuments on the battlefield, but as the bitterness of the conflict faded, the battlefield changed, too. The War Department began to erect tablets marking Confederate positions in the late 1890s. The first monument to a Confederate regiment, the 2nd Maryland Infantry CSA, was dedicated in 1886 at Culp's Hill.

Alabama State Monument: Located on South Confederate Avenue, the Alabama Monument stands where a brigade of troops began their assault toward Little Round Top on July 2.

In addition to regimental monuments, memorials from most states that fought at Gettysburg were erected. The Virginia Memorial was the first state memorial to honor Confederate soldiers. Completed in 1917, it features General Lee astride his favorite horse, Traveller. Other notable state monuments include the elaborate Pennsylvania Monument, the only memorial to record all the soldiers from that state who participated in the battle, and the Maryland Monument, which features bronze figures of a wounded Union and Confederate soldier side by side.

With its towering equestrian statues, the battlefield also honors many Confederate and Union Civil War generals—including George G. Meade, John F. Reynolds, John Sedgwick, Winfield S. Hancock, Oliver O. Howard, Henry Slocum, and James Longstreet. A few lower-ranking soldiers are memorialized, too. Only two civilians are honored with a statue at Gettysburg: Elizabeth Thorn, who buried dozens of soldiers at Evergreen Cemetery while her caretaker husband was off at war, and John Burns. A 69-year-old veteran of the War of 1812, Burns took up his musket, walked to the battlefield, and fought beside the members of the Iron Brigade. He was injured in battle and became a national hero. His monument was dedicated on July 1, 1903, the 40th anniversary of the battle.

Cemetery Ridge: Erected on July 4, 1891, this monument to the 72nd Pennsylvania Volunteer Infantry Regiment stands at the High Water Mark on Cemetery Ridge, near the copse of trees where the fighting peaked during Pickett's Charge.

Today, Gettysburg National Military Park preserves one of the world's largest collections of outdoor sculpture and monuments. It also contains markers that indicate the locations of the two armies' headquarters, and Confederate and Union tablets that relate the actions of every corps, division, brigade, and battery. Nearly 1,400 statues, monuments, markers, and tablets stand where the men fought.

Stevens Knoll: Monuments to Major General Henry W. Slocum and the 5th Maine Battery, 1st Corps, stand along Stevens Knoll, a ridge that stretches between Culp's Hill and Cemetery Hill.

General Robert E. Lee was one of the most famous leaders of the Civil War. Under his command, the Confederate army exploited Union mismanagement on numerous battlefields, making him the most victorious commander in the Confederacy.

General Lee: A bronzed statue of Robert E. Lee on his horse, Traveller, stands atop the Virginia Memorial, dedicated in 1917.

Born on January 19, 1807, in Westmoreland County, Virginia, he was the son of Anne Hill and Henry Lee, a distinguished cavalry officer during the American Revolution. Lee fought in the War with Mexico, serving in the U.S. Army for 32 years. At the outbreak of the Civil War, he declined an offer to command the Union army, instead opting to serve his native state. He worked in several administrative and field positions before being assigned to command the Confederate army at Richmond, which he named the "Army of Northern Virginia."

> *As far as I can judge there is nothing to be gained by this army remaining quietly on the defensive.*
>
> —General Robert E. Lee, June 8, 1863

Lee was known for being generous and affable, even in defeat. After the disastrous Pickett's Charge, he comforted George Pickett. "This has been my fight, and upon my shoulders rests the blame," he told General Pickett. "The men and officers of your command have written the name of Virginia as high today as it has ever been written before." Today, Lee's statue atop the Virginia Memorial overlooks the fields where 12,000 Confederates began their fateful charge.

General George Gordon Meade

General George Gordon Meade was a career army officer who fought in the Seminole Wars and the War with Mexico. Born in Cadiz, Spain, on December 31, 1815, General Meade offered his services to Pennsylvania at the outbreak of the Civil War. Meade gained a reputation for being short-tempered with junior officers and superiors alike, earning him the nickname "The Old Snapping Turtle." At the Battle of Glendale on June 30, 1862, he was seriously wounded—but he remained on the field, directing his troops until he was so weak from loss of blood that he could not remain in his saddle.

Meade recovered and was placed in command of the division of Pennsylvania Reserves before being promoted to command the 5th Army Corps. On June 28, 1863, Meade was placed in command of the Army of the Potomac. It was a position he assumed with some anxiety. On June 29, he wrote his wife, "You know how reluctant we both have been to see me placed in this position . . . [But] I had nothing to do but to accept and exert my utmost abilities to command success."

Meade is honored by two memorials in Gettysburg National Military Park, including an equestrian statue by Henry Kirke Bush-Brown, located near the site of Pickett's Charge.

General Meade: Seated on his horse, Old Baldy, Meade is memorialized today on Cemetery Ridge.

Meade's Hat: General George Meade wore this hat on his campaigns during the Civil War.

The Edward McPherson farm is situated on Chambersburg Road, one half mile west of Gettysburg. Although comprised primarily of pasture, the farm has two ridges that run perpendicular to Chambersburg Pike. Various monuments, including several to Pennsylvania's famed "Bucktail Brigade" and one to Union General John Reynolds, are stationed along McPherson's Ridge.

Union Brigadier General John Buford is also memorialized near the McPherson farm. On the morning of July 1, Buford's cavalrymen were in position near the farm when they learned that Confederate troops were approaching from the west. Buford established his main line along McPherson's Ridge and placed part of his artillery battery near the barn, on either side of Chambersburg Pike. Within hours, they were engaged in battle. Buford's outnumbered troops held the Confederates until Union General John Reynolds's infantry arrived, throwing back the Southerners in a furious counterattack. Reynolds was struck by a bullet during the battle and died instantly.

General Buford: Buford's statue, erected in 1892, stands along Chambersburg Pike. One of the gun tubes at the base of his monument fired the first Union shell at the Battle of Gettysburg.

McPherson Farm: After the battle, Confederate surgeons used the McPherson buildings as a temporary hospital. Today, only the barn remains.

That afternoon, Colonel Roy Stone's Bucktail Brigade positioned itself around the McPherson farm. These Pennsylvania soldiers—named because of the deer tails affixed to their caps—were attacked by Confederates advancing from the north and west. A furious battle ensued. After two hours of fighting, Stone's brigade had lost more than half its men and was forced to retreat to Seminary Ridge. There, the Bucktail Brigade made one final stand before retreating to Cemetery Hill.

They will attack you in the morning and will come booming . . . You will have to fight like the devil to hold your own.

—Union General John Buford to Colonel Thomas Devin, June 30, 1863

Many soldiers on both sides considered John Reynolds to be the best general in the Union army. In early June 1863, Reynolds was offered the command of the Army of the Potomac, but he declined. When George Meade was appointed commander several weeks later, he asked Reynolds to lead one wing of the army: the three corps closest to Gettysburg.

> *Forward, men!*
> *Forward, for God's sake!*
>
> —The last words of Union General John F. Reynolds, July 1, 1863

Reynolds was from Lancaster, Pennsylvania, just 50 miles from Gettysburg, so the battle was a defense of his home state. Yet Reynolds did not live to see the battle unfold. On the morning of July 1, 1863, he rode behind the 2nd Wisconsin Infantry, watching them scramble into the woods next to the

The Death of Reynolds: Union General John Reynolds died on July 1, 1863, during the fighting on McPherson's Ridge. Reynolds is the officer on the horse in the back left, directly in front of the flag.

Bullets: A bullet like this struck General John Reynolds in the right temple, killing him instantly.

General Reynolds: An equestrian statue of Reynolds was built along Chambersburg Pike in 1899.

Edward McPherson farm. As he turned to locate his other troops, Reynolds slumped in his saddle, hit by a Confederate bullet. He was the highest-ranking officer on either side killed during the Battle of Gettysburg.

News of Reynolds's death sent shockwaves through the Union army. Meade later called Reynolds "one of the noblest souls among men, one of the most accomplished officers of this army." His body was taken behind the lines to the George House, which still stands in Gettysburg.

Today, several sculptures in Gettysburg National Military Park pay tribute to General Reynolds: an equestrian statue on McPherson's Ridge, a statue by John Quincy Adams Ward inside the Soldiers' National Cemetery, and a bronze figure along the base of the Pennsylvania Memorial.

A former constable of Gettysburg and a veteran of the War of 1812, John Burns had a reputation for cantankerousness. Burns lived with his wife on Chambersburg Street, on the western edge of Gettysburg. When the fighting on the first day drew near, the elderly veteran walked toward the sound of the guns to join the Union soldiers on the front lines of McPherson's Ridge. Burns brought his old powder horn and a smoothbore musket. Eventually, he found a place with the 7th Wisconsin Infantry in Herbst Woods, where they lent him a rifle.

Citizen Soldier: John Burns poses with his musket in front of his house on Chambersburg Street while recuperating from his wounds after the Battle of Gettysburg.

Burns was wounded three times, captured, and released by the Confederates. After the battle, he was a hero, posing for photographs, signing autographs, and appearing on the cover of national magazines. In November 1863, he met Abraham Lincoln on the president's trip to dedicate the Soldiers' National Cemetery. Burns was the first person in Gettysburg that the president had stated he wanted to meet.

My thanks are specially due to . . . John Burns, who, although over seventy years of age, shouldered his musket, and offered his services.

—Union Major General Abner Doubleday, in an official report on the Battle of Gettysburg, December 14, 1863

Powder Horn: Burns brought his old powder horn and smoothbore musket to fight the Confederates. He eventually found a place in Herbst Woods with the 7th Wisconsin Infantry. They lent him a rifle.

Burns Cottage: After Burns died, his Gettysburg home was demolished, inspiring veterans of the battle to do something to commemorate his services.

John Burns died in 1872 and is buried in Evergreen Cemetery. After his death, veterans of the battle proposed a memorial to commemorate his services. A sculpture of a defiant Burns was funded by the state of Pennsylvania and placed on McPherson's Ridge next to Herbst Woods. It was dedicated on July 1, 1903, the 40th anniversary of the battle.

Walking Toward War: This monument to John Burns stands on a boulder taken from the battlefield.

Oak Hill was an important position for the Confederates on July 1. Owned by John Forney, it had an expansive apple orchard on its southern slope. The hill's elevation allowed Confederate artillery to barrage Union troops on Seminary and McPherson ridges, while its woods provided concealment for Confederate infantry.

Eternal Light Peace Memorial: President Franklin Delano Roosevelt was the featured speaker at the dedication of the Eternal Light Peace Memorial. "All of them we honor," he said of the troops, "not asking under which flag they fought then, [but] thankful that they stand together under one flag now."

Around noon, Confederate gunners set up artillery in the orchard and opened fire on Union soldiers one half mile south. At 1:30 p.m., Confederate infantry, under General Robert Rodes, attacked. They were repulsed, encountering stiff Union resistance along nearby Oak Ridge and suffering devastating losses. Rodes then reorganized, brought up his reserves, and renewed his attack. Eventually, the Confederates forced the Union troops to abandon Oak Ridge.

Today, the Eternal Light Peace Memorial towers over Oak Hill. Surrounded by guns that mark the Confederate artillery positions, it rises 47 feet. Veterans from both sides proposed the memorial during the 1913 anniversary and reunion at Gettysburg, but it wasn't completed until the 75th anniversary of the battle in 1938.

Named for the Lutheran Theological Seminary, Seminary Ridge runs south and southeast, intersecting Emmitsburg Road. The ridge was a critical anchor for the Confederates on July 2 and 3, allowing General Lee and his men to observe the distant Union line, bombard the Union army on Cemetery Hill, and act as a screen when shifting his troops. The Confederates occupied the ridge late on the afternoon of July 1, and extended their lines north in a U-shape through Gettysburg and then east on Hanover Road. These lines matched the formation of the Union army, which was positioned on Culp's and Cemetery hills and south to Cemetery Ridge and Little Round Top.

North Carolina Memorial: On this stone marker is a tribute to the North Carolina soldiers of the Confederacy who "displayed heroism unsurpassed, sacrificing all in support of their cause."

North Carolina Monument: Dedicated in 1929, the North Carolina monument depicts a wounded officer pointing his troops toward the enemy.

Lee decided to strike the Army of the Potomac on both its left and right flanks on July 2, holding most of General A.P. Hill's corps on Seminary Ridge as reinforcements. Events escalated the following day during Pickett's Charge, when Confederate regiments marched from the ridge to attack the Union center along Cemetery Ridge.

General A. P. Hill: Hill, one of Lee's best generals, was assigned command of a newly formed corps after Stonewall Jackson's death in May 1863.

Virginia Memorial: The Virginia Memorial overlooks the fields of Pickett's Charge, where thousands of Confederate soldiers marched toward Union forces on Cemetery Ridge. Today, visitors can retrace those steps, beginning near the Virginia Memorial at Spangler Woods and ending at the High Water Mark.

Now, West Confederate Avenue winds through Seminary Ridge. Constructed at the turn of the century, the road is lined with markers to Confederate brigades and artillery batteries. Almost 80 artillery pieces, including many original guns, mark the location of various Confederate units. Most of the monuments erected by Southern states are also here, including memorials from North Carolina, Tennessee, Florida, Georgia, Mississippi, South Carolina, Alabama, and Virginia, which proudly displays an equestrian statue of General Lee.

General James Longstreet

One of the most recent memorials erected on the battlefield is the monument to Confederate General James Longstreet on Seminary Ridge. Dedicated in 1998, the statue is situated at ground level and captures Longstreet on horseback, leaning toward West Confederate Avenue. Longstreet grew to become one of the more controversial personalities of the Civil War both on and off the battlefield. During the Battle of Gettysburg, Longstreet was famously reluctant to order Pickett's Charge. Overcome with emotion, Longstreet gave his assent while sitting on a fence in a wooded section of Seminary Ridge. He later wrote that he could only drop his chin to his chest to indicate that General Pickett should advance toward what Longstreet believed was a lost cause. After the war, Longstreet joined the Republican Party. This was unpopular with Southerners, who held the party responsible for pursuing the war against the South and for its reconstruction policies—particularly those that gave rights to the newly freed slaves.

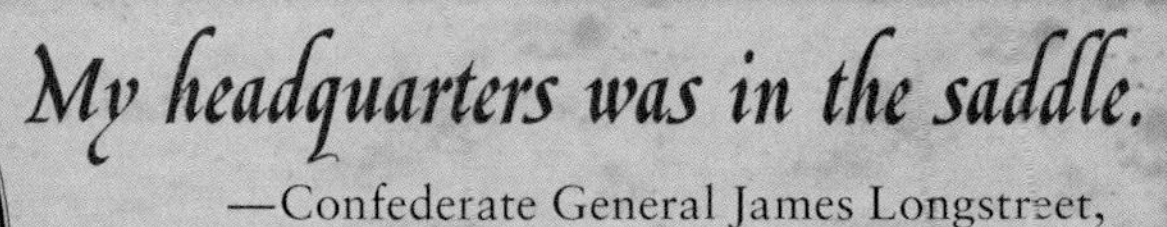

—Confederate General James Longstreet, referring to his role at the Battle of Gettysburg

General Longstreet: Longstreet admittedly spent very little time at his headquarters on Warfield Ridge, preferring to remain mobile during the battle.

In the post-war era, discussions swirled as to where the South went wrong. Soon the attention centered on the Battle of Gettysburg. Robert E. Lee refused to join in the debate, dying in 1870 without any response. But many Southern political leaders and former generals argued that Longstreet had not supported General Lee's wishes at Gettysburg as fully as he should have. Longstreet responded with criticisms of Lee's field decisions and strategy. Many Southerners held Lee's abilities as a commander in high regard and regarded Longstreet's comments as treachery. Although he was exonerated time and again by the many veterans who had marched, fought, and bled under his command, Longstreet remained at the center of bitter controversy until the day he died, January 2, 1904.

Pitzer's Woods: An equestrian statue of General Longstreet was dedicated in Pitzer's Woods, along Seminary Ridge.

General James Longstreet

Little Round Top is one of the most heavily visited sites in the park. The stone walls and barricades built by Union brigades still line the hill, and behind them stand monuments to its defenders, including a memorial to the 140th New York Infantry.

Little Round Top: The Confederates attacked Little Round Top on July 2, 1863, but were repelled by the Union's 5th Corps.

Unlike the thickly wooded Big Round Top, the smaller hill—located at the southern end of Cemetery Ridge—had been partially cleared of trees about a year before the battle. Strewn with large boulders, it gave Union forces a commanding view of the north and west, making it a key anchor for the Northern army. On the afternoon of July 2, Little Round Top was unoccupied by Union soldiers except for a signal station on its summit. While Longstreet's corps prepared to attack the Union's left flank, General Gouverneur K. Warren, the chief engineer of the Union army, arrived on the hill to assess the situation.

Warren's Telescope: This telescope belonged to Union General Gouverneur Warren. He may have used it to watch the Confederates approach Little Round Top.

Warren was aghast at what he saw: Union General Dan Sickles had moved his entire 3rd Corps out to the Devil's Den–Peach Orchard line, leaving Little Round Top unprotected. General Warren realized that the Confederates were headed toward the Round Tops and quickly called upon the 5th Corps for reinforcements. For nearly an hour, the Army of Northern Virginia poured deadly fire into the corps. The fighting became desperate as the Confederates began to overwhelm the Union line. At a critical point in the battle, Colonel Patrick O'Rorke arrived with his 140th New York Infantry and attacked. O'Rorke was killed, but his men drove the Confederates back and helped save the hill.

Cipher Disk: The Union army set up signal stations at strategic locations such as Culp's Hill, Cemetery Hill, and Little Round Top. With cipher disks like this, Union signalmen were able to encode messages to keep the enemy from reading important correspondence.

Gouverneur Warren: Swift action by Brigadier General Gouverneur K. Warren saved the Union army's key position on Little Round Top the afternoon of July 2, 1863.

Devil's Den

Devil's Den lies at the end of a ridge that separates Plum Run Valley from the Wheatfield. During the Battle of Gettysburg, the high ridge extending northwest from Devil's Den provided height and cover for the Union's 4th New York Battery. The Den's giant boulders also made it difficult for troops to move through the area, helping to protect the battery from attack.

Devil's Den: The Den's unique terrain presented challenges for both armies. One Southerner explained, "Large rocks from six to fifteen feet high are thrown together in confusion over a considerable area."

Union Captain James Smith hoped the Confederates would attack on the west side and not from another direction. On the afternoon of July 2, however, Smith was attacked from the front, flank, and eventually from his rear.

> *No troops could stand long in such a storm.*
>
> —Union soldier, 124th New York Infantry, at Devil's Den

The fight was brutal. Both sides had their battle formations fragmented by the rock piles and large boulders at the base of the Den. Officers lost control of their commands, and soldiers lost their way in the shower of bullets, shell, and canister. Smith was forced to abandon three of his cannon when the Confederates overran his position. The Confederates swarmed the summit, their sharpshooters practicing on Union targets over on Little Round Top.

After the battle, the area between Devil's Den and the Round Tops was nicknamed "The Slaughter Pen," and Plum Run Valley was referred to as the "Valley of Death." Today, a monument to Captain Smith and his 4th New York Battery stands on the ridge of the Den.

The Wheatfield

The Wheatfield, owned by farmer John Rose, consisted of approximately 20 acres of fully ripened wheat surrounded on three sides by Rose's woodlot. It became the scene of some of Gettysburg's fiercest fighting. In three hours on July 2, the two armies suffered more than 4,000 casualties.

Bordered by woods, the Wheatfield provided cover for Confederates maneuvering around the Union army. Veterans compared the battle there to a whirlpool—a stream of eddies and tides, attacks and counterattacks. The fighting finally ended when Union General Samuel Crawford led an evening counterattack that stopped the Confederates' advance. After the war, Crawford bought the land his troops had defended.

The Irish Brigade: This Celtic cross honors the New York members of the Irish Brigade who lost their lives at the Wheatfield on July 2.

One of Gettysburg's most memorable monuments is set in these woods. Dedicated to the three New York regiments of the "Irish Brigade," the green granite monument is topped by a Celtic cross and a life-sized sculpture of an Irish wolfhound, the traditional Irish symbol of loyalty.

Much of the Irish Brigade was comprised of immigrants who had come to the United States to escape political repression and the Potato Famine of the 1850s. The brigade fought with great distinction and great gallantry in previous Civil War battles, but by the opening of the Gettysburg campaign, it barely mustered 530 men. Almost 200 of them became casualties in the Wheatfield and adjacent woods.

Father William Corby was chaplain of the Union's famous Irish Brigade. On the afternoon of July 2 he stood on a large boulder and granted general absolution to more than 300 Catholic soldiers. Raising his voice above the din of battle, Father Corby comforted the young men who knelt before him, about to face death. The brigade was in the thick of battle at the Wheatfield within the hour.

Granting Absolution: This monument to the popular chaplain of the Irish Brigade, Father William Corby, stands near the George Weikert Farm.

After the war, Corby returned to teaching at Notre Dame University and was appointed university president. He took a brief appointment at Sacred Heart College in Watertown, Wisconsin, before coming back to Notre Dame in 1877. The university flourished under his guidance until his retirement in 1881. Father William Corby died in 1897 and was buried at Notre Dame. In 1910, a statue of the priest was erected upon the boulder where he stood.

The Peach Orchard, owned by Joseph Sherfy, lay at the intersection of Wheatfield and Emmitsburg roads. On high ground overlooking various farm fields, it was an important tactical location for the Union army. Four Union batteries were initially posted at the Peach Orchard on July 2 to strengthen the line taken up by General Dan Sickles. From there, the batteries bombarded Southern troops on Seminary Ridge and Warfield Ridge, and fired on the Confederates crossing the Rose Farm to attack the Wheatfield.

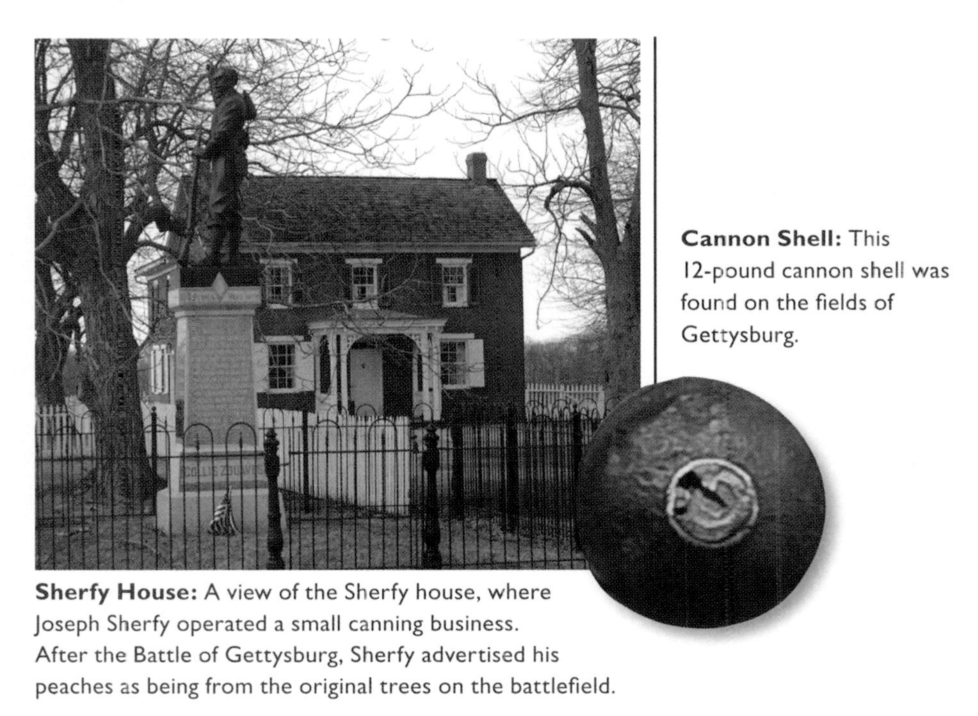

Cannon Shell: This 12-pound cannon shell was found on the fields of Gettysburg.

Sherfy House: A view of the Sherfy house, where Joseph Sherfy operated a small canning business. After the Battle of Gettysburg, Sherfy advertised his peaches as being from the original trees on the battlefield.

Confederate artillery opened up on the Union troops at the Peach Orchard about 3:30 p.m. Colonel E. P. Alexander said of the Confederate attack, "I thought that if ever I could overwhelm and crush them, I would do it now." He shelled the Union line for about 30 minutes. Union infantrymen from New Hampshire, Massachusetts, New Jersey, and Pennsylvania formed a line to protect the Union batteries near the orchard, but ultimately, a fierce attack by Confederate General William Barksdale's brigade broke their line and overran the Peach Orchard.

Joseph Sherfy's orchards were ruined during the battle—his fences were torn apart by Union troops and Confederate artillerymen, his crops trampled. On July 3, a shell caught his barn on fire, killing a number of Union wounded who were sheltered inside. A monument to the 114th Pennsylvania Infantry was erected on July 2, 1886, in front of Sherfy's house on Emmitsburg Road. The house still stands there today.

Union General Dan Sickles was on his mount, watching the July 2 battle at the Peach Orchard when a Confederate shell tore into his leg. His staff applied a tourniquet to stop the flow of blood and placed him on a blanket. In shock and fearing that he would be captured, Sickles was carried to an ambulance and driven to a field hospital on Baltimore Pike. That evening, an army surgeon removed General Sickles's shattered leg, effectively ending his career as a corps commander.

Hell, the whole battlefield is my monument.

—Union General Dan Sickles, when asked about not having a monument at Gettysburg, 1913

General Sickles: Sickles stands near Trostle Farm, where he lost his leg on the second day of the battle. The colorful general met author Mark Twain after the war, who is said to have quipped of Sickles, "He seemed to value the leg he lost over the leg he had."

Sickles visited Gettysburg many times after the war. An active supporter of the Gettysburg Battlefield Memorial Association, his interest in the development and care of the battlefield never waned. Sickles went on to represent the state of New York in congress, introducing the bill to establish Gettysburg National Military Park and transferring the property to the federal government in 1895. His last visit to Gettysburg was as a special guest during the 50th anniversary and reunion in 1913. He died on May 3, 1914, and was buried in Arlington National Cemetery. A granite marker now stands at the site where General Sickles was wounded.

A substantial hill with heavily wooded slopes, Culp's Hill was a perfect anchor for the Union's right flank at Gettysburg, the point of the famous "fishhook." There, local farmers had grazed animals in the woods and actively managed the woodlot so that it consisted primarily of mature oak, maple, and chestnut trees. During the night of July 1 and throughout the next day, the Union soldiers felled some of these trees to build a strong line of earthen and log defenses called breastworks. The remains of these breastworks still exist, marking the Union battle line.

Culp's Hill: On the night of July 2, Brigadier General George Sears Greene and his men successfully held the right flank of the Union army on Culp's Hill.

Late in the afternoon of July 2, most of the Union's 12th Corps left Culp's Hill to reinforce the left flank of the army. They left behind only a single brigade of New York regiments commanded by General George S. Greene. At dusk, three brigades of Confederate infantrymen attacked Greene's troops. The breastworks protected the outnumbered New Yorkers and helped them hold their position until nearly 10:00 p.m. After midnight, the rest of the 12th Corps returned, and the battle resumed early on July 3. For seven hours the battle raged, but by 11:00 a.m., the Confederates had been unable to make any headway. They withdrew, leaving Culp's Hill in Union hands.

With its bullet-ridden trees and expansive lines of breastworks, Culp's Hill became a popular destination after the war. Today, it is the site of numerous monuments, including the 2nd Maryland Infantry CSA Monument—the first to honor a Confederate regiment—and several dedicated to the regiments of Greene's brigade.

Located at the southern end of Culp's Hill, Spangler's Spring is adjacent to an open pasture area and is one of the battlefield's most well-known landmarks. On July 2, the Union 12th Corps occupied the land on Culp's Hill and Spangler's Spring, building breastworks and filling their canteens until being called to reinforce the embattled 3rd Corps at the Peach Orchard that afternoon. After the Union soldiers left, Confederate troops stumbled upon the spring and took possession of the area. Heavy fighting broke out when the 12th Corps returned that night. Union troops attacked the Confederates positioned near the spring, but were repulsed with heavy losses. Later in the morning, however, the Confederates withdrew, and Culp's Hill and Spangler's Spring were back in Union hands.

Spangler's Spring: The U.S. War Department built a permanent structure around the stream in 1895 to protect it from visitors.

After the battle, legend sprouted that the soldiers called temporary truces so both armies could fill their cups and canteens from the spring. Most likely these truces never occurred, due to the location of the spring and the vicious fighting that raged around it. The story probably originated from veterans who visited the battlefield years after the war when tales of cooperation were popular.

Still, this legend and history has made Spangler's Spring one of the most visited areas of the park. In 1895, to protect the stream, the United States War Department constructed a permanent stone and concrete cover with a small metal trap door so visitors could gain access to the waters. For several years, the park also provided a metal dipper for visitors to quench their thirst as the soldiers had done years before. But this practice was halted due to the possibility of ground water contamination.

East Cemetery Hill

Situated on the southern edge of Gettysburg and overlooking the town, East Cemetery Hill is one of the premier landmarks of the battlefield. At the time of the battle, Cemetery Hill—named because of Evergreen Cemetery perched on its summit—was divided into small pastures bordered by stone walls. On July 1, the Union's 11th Corps claimed the hill, positioning themselves behind stone walls and constructing earthen barricades or "lunettes" to protect their cannon farther up the hill. Later that day, other Union regiments, battered from the first day's fighting, regrouped there. General Winfield Scott Hancock spent the afternoon rallying and reorganizing these troops, and by the morning of July 2, Cemetery Hill was one of the most heavily defended positions on the field.

East Cemetery Hill: One of the first portions of land purchased by the Gettysburg Battlefield Memorial Association after the Battle of Gettysburg was East Cemetery Hill. The association replanted grass and rebuilt stone walls to restore the hill to its pre-battle landscape.

Despite the hill's apparent invincibility, Confederate troops briefly shattered the Union defenses at dusk on July 2. The night turned thick with smoke and gunfire, and many Union soldiers fled up the hill with the Confederates in pursuit. At the summit, the fighting turned hand to hand as Union artillerymen fought to protect their guns. But Union reserves soon arrived and staged a counterattack, and by midnight, Cemetery Hill was considered secure.

Shortly after the Battle of Gettysburg, the Gettysburg Battlefield Memorial Association purchased the eastern portion of Cemetery Hill, rebuilding stone fences, planting grass, and preserving the artillery lunettes. The association also placed surplus cannon on stone pedestals in the artillery positions and sponsored the construction of a wooden observation tower. Today, with cannon sprinkled throughout rolling pastures, East Cemetery Hill is one of the battlefield's most picturesque sites.

On July 3, General Lee tasked General James Longstreet with commanding the infantry in the final assault on Union troops known today as Pickett's Charge. After a massive military bombardment, some 12,000 Confederates began the long march toward the Union line. As they reached Emmitsburg Road, they were startled by blasts from hundreds of Union muskets. Confederate leadership melted away as sergeants replaced fallen lieutenants and captains, urging the men on.

Pennsylvania Memorial: The largest state monument at Gettysburg National Military Park is the Pennsylvania Memorial, located at Cemetery Ridge.

The assault faltered at nearly all the points along the Confederate front, but at the angle in a stone wall along Cemetery Ridge, one group of about 200 Confederate soldiers led by General Lewis Armistead desperately rushed into the Union position. The fighting was fierce, taking place just yards apart, but the Union's firepower turned the tide. Armistead fell mortally wounded. Those with him were shot down, surrendered, or retreated.

High Water Mark: This small "copse" or grove of trees was the site of the point-blank fighting that occurred during the climax of Pickett's Charge—the Confederate army's high point of the Civil War.

Cemetery Ridge marks the Confederate crest of the battle. Called the High Water Mark of the Rebellion, it is one of the most visited sites on the battlefield. It has also been the scene of countless reunions and ceremonies—including several visits by veterans from Pickett's division and the Philadelphia brigade, who returned to shake hands over the stone wall.

Generals Lewis Armistead and Winfield Hancock

General Lewis Armistead was commissioned as a second lieutenant in the infantry in 1839. He served in the Mexican War, earning two brevets for bravery. At the beginning of the Civil War, Armistead—a native of Virginia—offered his services to the Confederacy. In doing so, he was forced to sever ties with his closest friend: Union General Winfield Hancock. According to some accounts, Armistead vowed at his Union farewell party, "If I should ever lift a hand against Hancock in battle, may God strike me dead."

Both men played important roles in the Battle of Gettysburg. Armistead was a brigadier general and commanded an infantry brigade under Major General George G. Pickett. During Pickett's Charge, Armistead was mortally wounded while leading his men over the stone wall. Hancock, who led the 2nd Corps of the Union army, was also wounded while directing Vermont troops in a counterattack on Pickett's men.

Friend to Friend Memorial: This Masonic memorial depicts Union Captain Bingham assisting Confederate General Armistead on the battlefield of Pickett's Charge.

On the battlefield, Armistead asked Hancock's aide, Union Captain Henry Bingham, to deliver his personal effects to Hancock. Armistead was taken to the field hospital at Spangler Farm. He died the next morning. Hancock's injury forced him to leave the army until the following year, 1864. After the war, he received accolades from Congress for his role in the Battle of Gettysburg.

To commemorate Armistead and Hancock's friendship, the Friend to Friend Memorial was erected in the National Cemetery Annex in 1993. Hancock is memorialized by several monuments in the park, including an equestrian statue on Cemetery Ridge; a marker along Hancock Avenue, where he was wounded; and a statue on the Pennsylvania Memorial. Armistead is also honored by a memorial on Cemetery Ridge: a scroll-topped granite monument marking the location where he was mortally wounded. Erected by friends of the Armistead family in 1887, it was the first monument to a Confederate officer placed at Gettysburg.

One of the first truly "national" cemeteries, the Soldiers' National Cemetery is located on the southern edge of Gettysburg and is part of Gettysburg National Military Park. The idea for the cemetery was conceived by several different individuals shortly after the battle. Approximately 7,000 soldiers were buried in and around the town, and the heavy rains after the battle had exposed many of the hastily dug graves.

Representing the state of Pennsylvania, and with the financial support of the Northern states represented at Gettysburg, local attorney David Wills purchased 17 acres on Cemetery Hill, adjacent to the Evergreen Cemetery. He then commissioned William Saunders as the landscape architect. Saunders decided that the design should express a "simple grandeur," and created a semicircular plan with soldiers from each state buried together in distinct sections. After the blueprints were in place, Wills began to grapple with how to bring the thousands of bodies from the battlefield to the cemetery. He advertised for proposals to rebury the dead. The winning bid, from Samuel Weaver of Gettysburg, was $1.59 per body.

The Soldiers' National Cemetery: Many of the Union soldiers who were killed at the Battle of Gettysburg are buried at the Soldiers' National Cemetery.

The cemetery committee's work was still incomplete when the cemetery was formally dedicated on November 19, 1863. By the end of the war, 3,555 Union soldiers were buried at the Soldiers' National Cemetery, 1,664 of them unknowns. The cemetery was finally completed in 1869 after the installation of grave markers, a stone-chipped walk, and the Soldiers' National Monument, which stands in the center of the grounds.

Gettysburg Cemetery: An 1882 view of the Soldiers' National Cemetery shows many of the trees that were planted by the U.S. government. The Soldiers' National Monument is in the distance.

In 1872, the cemetery's administration was turned over to the federal government. The United States War Department paved walkways through the cemetery, planted many of the decorative trees that adorn the cemetery grounds, and commissioned tablets with stanzas from Theodore O'Hara's poem "The Bivouac of the Dead." The cemetery was transferred to the National Park Service in 1933.

We have come to dedicate a portion of that field, as a final resting place for those who here gave their lives that that nation might live.

—Abraham Lincoln, Gettysburg Address, November 19, 1863

A number of post-war burials took place in the cemetery, and expansions occurred until 1968. The cemetery and cemetery annex now hold the graves of veterans from every major American war, including the Civil War, the Spanish-American War, World War I, World War II, Korea, and Vietnam. Today, the Soldiers' National Cemetery is one of the most honored and visited sites at Gettysburg National Military Park.

13th
MASS. VOLS.

Beyond the Battlefield

David Wills House

The home of Gettysburg attorney David Wills was situated near the center of Gettysburg. It was also the center of the immense clean-up process after the battle, and the place where President Lincoln put his finishing touches on the Gettysburg Address.

The Civil War came to Wills's doorstep when he saw "a group of rebels with an axe break open the store door" belonging to one of his tenants. Local citizens gathered in his cellar as the fighting raged around town. After the battle, Wills gathered and warehoused supplies for the wounded, and fought for compensation for the farmers who suffered losses. He also sought help from Pennsylvania Governor Andrew Curtin in taking care of Pennsylvania's dead. Curtin promptly designated Wills as a state agent and charged him with seeing to their proper burial.

David Wills House: Located in downtown Gettysburg, the David Wills House is a National Park Service Site. It was here that President Lincoln finished the Gettysburg Address.

The idea for establishing a permanent national cemetery for Union soldiers was presented during a meeting with other state agents at Wills's house. Governor Curtin approved the concept and gave Wills the authority to oversee its construction. David Wills invited President Abraham Lincoln to speak at the cemetery's dedication in November 1863 and hosted the president during his visit to Gettysburg. His other guests included featured speaker Edward Everett, Governor Curtin, and the French minister to Washington, D.C.

The David Wills House opened to the public on February 12, 2009, Abraham Lincoln's 200th birthday. The museum—a National Park Service Site and part of Gettysburg National Military Park—tells the story of Lincoln and the Gettysburg Address. It features six galleries, including two rooms that have been restored to their 1863 appearance: Wills's office, where he received letters from families looking for loved ones and began planning for the cemetery, and the bedroom where Lincoln stayed and prepared the Gettysburg Address.

Eisenhower Home: Located adjacent to the Gettysburg battlefield, the home of former president Dwight Eisenhower and his wife, Mamie, is now a National Historic Site. The site features walking tours of the farm and grounds, a home tour, a Junior Secret Service program, and several multimedia exhibits.

Eisenhower National Historic Site

Located adjacent to the Gettysburg battlefield, the Eisenhower National Historic Site features the only home ever owned by President Dwight D. Eisenhower and his wife, Mamie. The property served as a weekend retreat and retirement home for the Eisenhowers. With its peaceful setting and view of South Mountain, it created a respite from Washington and a backdrop for efforts to reduce Cold War tensions.

President Eisenhower's association with Gettysburg began in 1915, when he visited the site with his class at West Point. Three years later, during World War I, he took command of Camp Colt, located on the fields of Pickett's Charge. After serving in World War II, Eisenhower returned to Gettysburg. He and his wife, Mamie, bought a 189-acre farm adjoining the battlefield in 1950.

President Eisenhower used his weekends at Gettysburg to relax, but he also held meetings with his staff and entertained a steady stream of dignitaries. He often gave world leaders a tour of his Angus herd and cattle barns before bringing them back to the house to sit on the porch. Eisenhower said the informal atmosphere of the porch allowed him to "get the other man's equation."

In 1961, General and Mrs. Eisenhower retired to their Gettysbug farm after 45 years of service to their country. The Eisenhowers donated their home and farm to the National Park Service in 1967. Two years later, Eisenhower died at the age of 78. Mrs. Eisenhower continued to live on the farm until her death in 1979. The National Park Service opened the site the following year.

After the battle, Gettysburg's farmers were eager to reclaim their fields. But to Union veterans, the battlefield came to represent all the battles of the war and the courage and sacrifice of their comrades. For them, it was a sacred place.

Within two weeks of the battle, Gettysburg lawyer David McConaughy purchased Steven's Knoll with the intention of building a memorial there. He also used his own money to buy portions of Cemetery Hill, Culp's Hill, and Little Round Top. In 1864, McConaughy and other citizens formed the Gettysburg Battlefield Memorial Association (GBMA) to preserve the scene of the battle. "There could be no more fitting and expressive memorial," said McConaughy, "than the battlefield itself, with its natural and artificial defenses preserved and perpetuated in the exact form and conditions as they were during the battle."

Commemorative Medal: This reunion badge was given to veterans on the 50th anniversary of the battle in 1913.

Veteran Reunion: These veterans returned to Gettysburg in 1913 for the largest combined reunion of Civil War veterans ever held.

The state authorized the GBMA to acquire land, make roads, and erect monuments, among other measures. By the 1870s, hundreds of Union veterans had joined the association, transforming it into a national organization with strong ties to the Grand Army of the Republic, the main Union veterans' group. The association purchased hundreds of acres of land and constructed more than 20 miles of new roads on the battlefield in the late 1800s and early 1900s.

GAR Encampment: Members of the Grand Army of the Republic (GAR), the Union's powerful veterans organization, camped on the fields of Gettysburg to celebrate the battle's 50th anniversary.

By 1890, more than 150,000 people visited the battlefield each year. The park experienced some growing pains when an electric railway company began laying tracks across the battlefield to carry tourists to Little Round Top in 1893. Veterans urged the company to stop; former Union general Dan Sickles even called the railway a "piece of vandalism." Ultimately, the Supreme Court ruled that the government had the authority to halt the railway.

The GBMA disbanded and deeded its land—about 522 acres—to the U.S. government in 1895. The government created Gettysburg National Military Park, making it a park for all Americans. At the same time, Union veterans came to a consensus that both sides of the story should be represented at the park. More Confederate veterans began to return to Gettysburg.

The War Department turned the Gettysburg battlefield over to the National Park Service in 1933. Tourism grew steadily after World War II and exploded after the battle's 100th anniversary in 1963. Today, the park has grown to about 6,000 acres and contains 26 miles of roads. Hundreds of thousands of visitors immerse themselves in the nation's history at Gettysburg every year.

General Sickles: In July 1913, Dan Sickles (seated) returned to Gettysburg for the last time to celebrate the 50th anniversary of the battle. He died the following year at the age of 95.

Founding Fathers

When the government established Gettysburg National Military Park in 1895, Congress appointed a three-man commission—all veterans of the battle—to oversee the park's development. The park commissioners relocated more than 300 cannon from arsenals across the country, mounted the tubes on new carriages, and placed them at the sites of batteries during the battle. They also hired a civil engineer to help with the huge task of development. The core of the park today—from trees and towers to roads and monuments—grew from the vision and labors of these four men:

John Nicholson served with the 28th Pennsylvania Infantry at the Battle of Gettysburg. In 1893, he was appointed chairman of the Gettysburg National Park Commission and guided the development of the park for nearly 30 years.

Union Captain Charles Richardson was wounded on the second day of the Battle of Gettysburg and discharged from the army in 1864. Thirty-one years later, he returned as one of the commissioners of the park.

William Robbins was a Confederate officer in the 4th Alabama Infantry and a congressman from North Carolina after the war. He tirelessly urged his comrades to attend reunions at Gettysburg and play a role in the future of the park. He also composed most of the tablets that still line Confederate Avenue.

Emmor B. Cope served in the Topographical Engineers during the Battle of Gettysburg. After the war, he was chief engineer at the park for almost 35 years and the last superintendent who was a veteran of the Civil War. Cope personally oversaw the creation of much of the park as it exists today, from roads and woodlots to cannon carriages and observation towers that he designed himself.

The government is slowly making of Gettysburg a most interesting and . . . instructive memorial of the great fight.

—*Harper's Weekly*, October 12, 1901

THE GETTYSBURG FOUNDATION

In 1989, the Gettysburg Foundation joined with the National Park Service to enhance preservation and understanding of America's most revered Civil War battlefield. The Foundation—which includes thousands of Friends of Gettysburg members nationwide—focuses on a broad mission that includes land, monument, cannon, and artifact preservation; battlefield rehabilitation; and education.

On behalf of the National Park Service, the Foundation raised money for, built, and now operates the Gettysburg National Military Park Museum and Visitor Center, which opened in 2008. The goals of the Museum and Visitor Center are to preserve the park's massive collection of Civil War artifacts and archival items; maintain the colossal *Battle of Gettysburg* Cyclorama painting; rehabilitate key portions of the battlefield (including the location of the park's former visitor facilities) by returning them to their 1863 appearance; and provide visitors with an inspiring experience that explains the Battle of Gettysburg within the context of the American Civil War and American history. The Gettysburg Foundation and the National Park Service are helping to preserve this consecrated ground as a classroom of democracy for future generations.

Fields of Pickett's Charge: Pickett's division was one of nine infantry divisions in the Army of Northern Virginia. During the brief charge, more than half of Pickett's troops were killed, wounded, or captured.

Gettysburg Friends: Thousands of Friends of Gettysburg get involved each year in preserving history by painting and building fences, restoring monuments, and donating money to support battlefield rehabilitation.

Education and Research

Gettysburg National Military Park offers a variety of resources for everyone from grade-school children to retirees. New materials for teachers include a field trip planning kit, "The Best Field Trip Ever!" and Civil War-replica "Traveling Trunks." There are also educational programs for Friends of Gettysburg members and nonmembers; special lectures and series for adults and students; satellite broadcast tours from Park Rangers; Junior Ranger and Junior Secret Service programs for kids; summer scholar programs for students; and living history programs in which volunteer organizations portray soldiers and civilians from the Civil War. Since 1915, the park has also offered educational tours from Licensed Battlefield Guides. These men and women in uniform have helped visitors understand the Battle of Gettysburg, offering accurate and enlightening tours of the battlefield both by car and on foot.

Supporting Gettysburg

At Gettysburg, the future of freedom hung in the balance. Now millions of people visit the battlefield and Museum and Visitor Center each year, immersing themselves in the history of the American Civil War. For more than two decades, the Friends of Gettysburg have worked to support battlefield preservation, donating money and volunteering their time at Gettysburg National Military Park. Today, with the National Park Service, the Gettysburg Foundation continues its mission to protect the battlefield and educate the public about the heritage and lasting significance of the Battle of Gettysburg.

Gettysburg National Military Park Museum and Visitor Center: Official Guidebook was developed by Beckon Books in cooperation with the Gettysburg Foundation and Event Network. Beckon Books is an imprint of FRP Books, 2451 Atrium Way, Nashville, Tennessee, 37214. Beckon publishes custom books for cultural attractions, corporations, and non-profit organizations. FRP, Inc. is a wholly owned subsidiary of Southwestern, Inc., Nashville, Tennessee.

Christopher G. Capen, *President, Beckon Books*
Monika Stout, *Design/Production*
Betsy Holt, *Writer/Editor*
www.beckonbooks.com
877-311-0155

Event Network is the retail partner of the Gettysburg National Military Park Museum and Visitor Center and is proud to benefit and support Gettysburg's mission to educate visitors on the significance of the Battle of Gettysburg.
www.eventnetwork.com

The Gettysburg Foundation is a private, nonprofit educational organization working in partnership with the National Park Service to enhance preservation and understanding of the heritage and lasting significance of Gettysburg.

Administrative Offices: 717-338-1243
Museum and Visitor Center Tickets: 877-874-2478
Tickets sales and other purchases in the Museum and Visitor Center benefit battlefield preservation.

WE COULD USE MORE FRIENDS. Join the Friends of Gettysburg and help preserve this hallowed ground for future generations.
www.gettysburgfoundation.org

ISBN: 978-1-935442-07-3
Printed in the United States of America
10 9 8 7 6 5 4 3 2 1

Map Credits
Brian Lemke/www.lemkedesign.com: *32–33, 52–53, 56, 59, 60, 65, 67, 73*

Photo Credits
NPS: *11, 13c, 16, 17, 24–25, 30a, 30b, 34, 38b, 39a, 39b, 40a, 40b, 41a, 41b, 47a, 47b, 48, 49, 54a, 57b, 61b, 64a, 64b, 67, 68b, 71b, 72, 74a, 74b, 76a, 77, 78–79, 80b, 81a, 81b, 82–83, 84a, 87a, 87b, 88a, 89, 90a, 90b, 91, 92a, 94b, 95, 96, 98b, 101b, 110, 111b, 113, 114, 115b, 117b, 121a, 126b, 127b, 131a, 131b, 134, 137, 142, 143, 144a*

Gettysburg Foundation: *1, 6–7, 10, 12b, 13b, 55, 92, 106, 107, 111a, 115a, 118–119, 120, 121b, 124–125, 127a, 130, 136a*

Sue Boardman/Gettysburg Foundation: *21, 22, 23a, 23b, 26a*

Ashley Wright: *4–5, 8–9, 152*

Dru Neil: *14, 104–105, 108, 122a, 126a, 129, 140–141, 148*

Michael Vyskocil: *138*

Library of Congress: *31, 35, 36, 37a, 37b, 38a, 42, 43, 44–45, 46, 50, 51, 54b, 57a, 58, 61a, 62a, 62b, 63, 66a, 66b, 68a, 69, 70–71, 75a, 75b, 84b, 85, 86, 88b, 93, 94a, 95, 97, 98a, 99, 100–101, 102, 103, 112, 116, 117a, 122b 123, 132, 139, 144b, 145, 146*

Bill Dowling: *12a, 13a, 18–19, 20, 26b, 27, 28–29, 149*

Event Network: *12c*

IWM Photography: cover, *2–3, 76b, 80a, 109, 128, 133, 135, 136b*

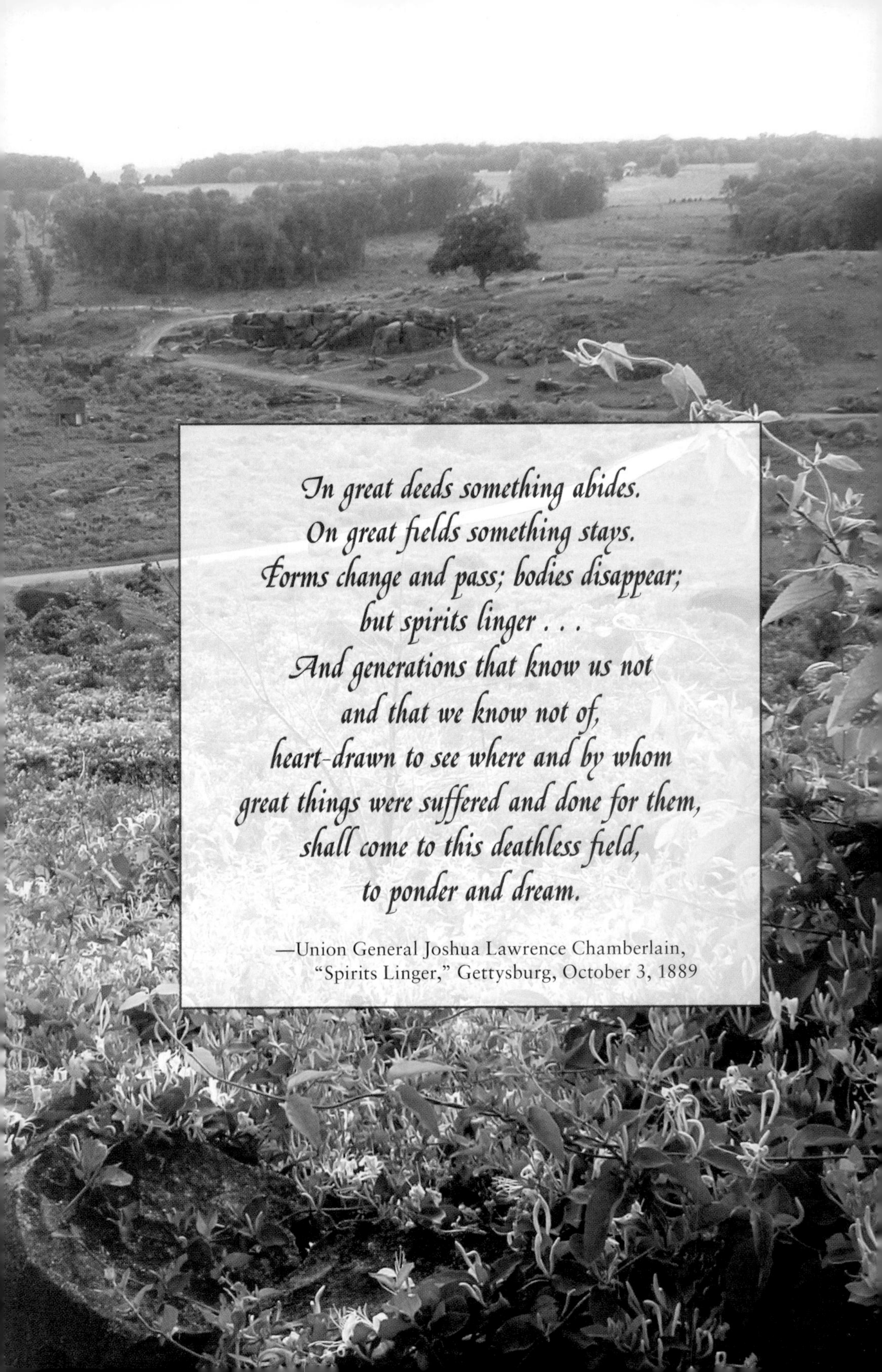

In great deeds something abides.
On great fields something stays.
Forms change and pass; bodies disappear;
but spirits linger . . .
And generations that know us not
and that we know not of,
heart-drawn to see where and by whom
great things were suffered and done for them,
shall come to this deathless field,
to ponder and dream.

—Union General Joshua Lawrence Chamberlain,
"Spirits Linger," Gettysburg, October 3, 1889